Mindfulness:

Living in the Moment

Living in the Breath

Mindfulness:

Living in the Moment Living in the Breath

By

Amit Ray, PhD

I L P

Inner Light Publishers
www.inner-light-in.com

Published

by

INNER LIGHT PUBLISHERS

www.inner-light-in.com

This Edition Published 2015

ISBN: 9789382123347

Email: innerlight.in@gmail.com

Table of Contents

INTRODUCTION 7

Live in the Moment - Stop Living on Autopilot 9
Breath : The Doorway to Consciousness 15
Living in the Breath - Use Breath as a Boat 16
A Simple Breath Exercise to Free your Mind 17
Compassion –The Mindful Attitude towards Life 19

PART – I: FOUNDATIONS OF MINDFULNESS 25

What is Mindfulness? 25
Adoring the Beauty of Life 27
Mindfulness: An Antidote to Mind-wandering 28
Mindfulness and the Scope for Planning and Creativity 31
Seven Factors of Mindfulness 33
1. Paying attention to the Present moment 34
2. Non-attached Witnessing 35
3. Gentleness and Compassion 36
4. Patience and Relaxation 39
5. Acceptance and Openness 41
6. Identifying and beautifying the experiences 43
7. Being Spacious and Non-reactive 45
Implementing Mindfulness: Four Small Steps 46
Hierarchy of Mindfulness : Basic Framework of Mindfulness 48
1. External Environmental Awareness: 51
2. Activity Awareness 55
3. Body Posture Awareness 56
4. Body Parts Awareness 57
5. Breathing Awareness 57
6. Body sensation awareness 58
7. Feelings awareness 59
8. Thought awareness 60
9. Awareness of mental states 62
10. Awakening factor awareness 63
11. Awareness of the being 64

12. Awareness of the Ultimate 64

PART II: MINDFULNESS OF DAILY ACTIVITIES **67**

1. Waking up in Mindfulness..68
2. Mindful Tooth Brushing..71
3. Taking the Shower Mindfully 74
4. Mindful Breathing 77
5. Mindful Driving 80
6. Mindfulness at Office 85
7. Mindful De-cluttering..96
8. Mindful Posture Awareness 102
9. Mindful Walking 114
10. Mindful Eating 117
11. Mindful Sleeping 119
12. Mindful Attitudes 121
13. Mindful Goal Setting and Planning 123

PART –II: MICRO-MINDFULNESS MEDITATION............................**127**

Micro-Mindfulness practices 131

1. Micro-Mindfulness: Five Deep Breathings *131*

2. Micro-Mindfulness: Awareness of the Things Around You *132*

3. Micro-Mindfulness with Earth Touching..........................*134*

PART IV:FORMAL MINDFULNESS MEDITATIONS **137**

1. Breath Meditation..137
2. Breath Meditation Type II..140
3. Mindfulness of Body Sensations 142
4. Feeling Awareness Meditation 146
5. Posture Meditation 149

PART V:FLOWERING OF MINDFULNESS......................................**153**

ABOUT THE AUTHOR **157**

ALSO FROM INNER LIGHT PUBLISHERS **158**

Introduction

Living in the moment - living in the breath is the backbone of mindfulness meditation. Living in the moment - living in the breath destroys the cyclic habitual pattern of stress, strain and anxieties. There is no other method which is so easy and so effective for stress management.

Suffering, anxiety, tension, fear, guilt, anger, and depression are the fabrics of common life. How to conquer them? In learning to overcome them lies the secret of happiness. Suffering arises due to the unaware momentum of life. Being carried away by such momentum is the cause of anxiety, fear and stress. Mindfulness brings control on that momentum. Mindfulness is also coming out of this momentum. Suffering also arises due to attachment and aversion to things. Mindfulness helps us to eliminate the attachments and aversions. It helps us to accept changes gently. If you want to conquer the anxieties of life, live in the moment, live in the breath. Peace and happiness exist in the moment. Heaven exists in the breath.

Mindfulness is accessing that heaven here and now.

Mindfulness is returning back to the source - where we are. Mindfulness is recognizing and welcoming the peace and beauty that is given to us by the existence in the present moment. Peace is flowing in our breath, in our blood, in the nature and in the whole existence.

Mind is like a net, drawn by the needles of past and future with the thread of desires and fears. Do not get caught up in your own net. Move freely over the net without getting stuck, like a spider. Mindfulness is the way for not getting stuck into the networks of thoughts.

Mind usually finds joy in chasing the future, which often brings stress. When flowers blossom, the fragrance spreads, and the bees come. Mindfulness brings the fragrance of peace, clarity, tranquility and compassion. Mindfulness is not chasing the bees but blossoming the flower with beauty and nectar for bees to come. When we chase something, we waste our energy. Mindfulness is not the path of chasing. It is the path of awareness and beautification. Always keep mindfulness as simple, easy and joyful. You can gain success by two ways: by chasing it with stress and tension, or by attracting success effortlessly. Mindfulness is the second one. Mindfulness minimizes the wastage of mental energy. Our choice lies in the present moment. Mindfulness enables us to attract positive energy, positive people and positive incidents in the present moment. Mindfulness opens the doors for more positive energy to enter our life.

Mindfulness makes us kind, fair, creative and focused. Mindfulness increases our adaptability, positive attitude and self-confidence. It brings us out from the old mental scripts into the ground realities. Mindfulness brings balance in life – balance between doubt and trust, patience and rush.

Live in the Moment - Stop Living on Autopilot

Life is a collection of moments. In every moment there are so many miracles around us, but we rarely notice them and we see them as ordinary. Mindfulness makes our ordinary moments extraordinary – full with the music of awareness, simplicity and happiness.

Mindfulness helps us understand the miracles of the moments. Look at the beauty in the smallest moments. Miracles are waiting for your attention. Looking at the beauty in the smallest moments will help you to stay in the present moment. Every moment has thousand one flowers – some are fresh – some are old. Every moment has ups and downs, light and darkness, happiness and challenges. Every moment has many roses with thorns. Focus your energy on the roses, and not on the thorns. Wherever we focus and wherever we pay our attention that grows. Mindfulness is focusing on the positive aspects of the moment with calmness and detachment. Human mind is complex and highly gifted. Mindfulness helps us reach a deeper state of the mind. Mindfulness offer insights into some of life's most difficult challenges.

Every moment life unfolds its wings slowly. Mindfulness is beautification of the moment. Beautification happens through attention, awareness, love and compassion. Every moment is fresh and every moment is new – focus on the beauty of the moment. Every moment comes with food to nourish our soul. Moment will soon vanish into another moment – into another universe and a new moment arises with new hopes, new challenges and new possibilities. Mindfulness is knowing the texture, color and fragrance of the moment in its totality. Adore the beauty of life. Through adoration of life, your consciousness becomes positive and life will be positive. Adore the beauty of breath. Through adoration of breath, your mind will become still. Do not try to hold on to the moment. Do not get attached to the experience of the moment. Let it flow, and be the observer. In this journey of life every moment is sacred; every experience is an opportunity to evolve. Every moment is an occasion to touch the divinity. Understanding life in the moment in its full form is the highest pilgrimage. Life is knocking at your door every moment – accept the moment with intelligence, awareness and kindness.

Each moment has positive elements and negative elements. Pay attention to the positive elements. Learn to choose your thoughts. You need to know the thoughts that drain your energy and the thoughts that motivate you and enhance your energy.

Even in the darkest moments – there are many stars on the sky. Mindfulness is focusing on the stars on background of darkness. Even the darkness has some beauty, calmness and nourishment for our soul. Moreover, darkness is never a permanent phenomenon; – like dew drops, darkness will evaporate as the morning sun rises.

Normally, we cannot appreciate the moment. We are often caught in the network of association - we are often lost in the network of thoughts and the moment slips away. Normally, we do not notice the sights, smells, sounds and tastes that we experience in each moment. We notice them only when there is some pain or unpleasant things. Normally, we do not give much value to the obvious peace elements of life. We do not have the time to aware about these. We are always busy with many so called important things of our life. Our ego, our intellect and our society do not give much value to these apparently simple things of life. We do not feel to notice the birds, the trees, the blue sky and many other things and events that nature is constantly presenting before us. We do not notice our body postures. We do not notice our thoughts. We are always preoccupied by our habitual thought patterns.

We are driven by the inertia of our habits. We have given the simple peace, beauty and bliss the last priority. We are motivated by our ego and intellect. We are living in a goal driven society. We are carried away by our thoughts. We do not know how to stop them. We react to a situation. We do not know how to respond with calmness and clarity of mind. We do not know much about our emotions and feelings. We do not know how our thoughts are controlling our emotions and behaviors. We are too much busy with the external world. We have a beautiful heart, but we do not have the time to cultivate that. Mindfulness makes us aware about the simple peace and beauty of life. Mindfulness helps us enjoy the life more, and understand ourselves better. It helps us to celebrate life in a meaningful way. It helps us to glorify the life, through the beauty of the present moment.

Mindfulness of the moment does not need much preparation. Anywhere and any moment you can practice it. Just willingness to practice and openness of heart is all that is required. You can apply mindfulness of the moment while engaged in your daily activities. You can practice mindfulness of the moment even when you are going through some difficulties and troubling experiences. Mindfulness of your breath makes the situation easier to handle, and when the experience is over, mindfulness of the moment makes it easier to let go and move on. Mindfulness of the moment gives you enormous freedom to move on with your life without clinging to the clutters of past experiences and negative thoughts associated with it. It is tremendously liberating. Mindfulness of the moment can liberate you from your Karmic debt. You don’t have to carry them on forever. Mindfulness is engaging your energy into the present moment. Mindfulness helps us to know ourselves - the patterns of our thoughts, our limitations, our likes, dislikes, worries, anxieties, wounds, pleasures, happiness and joys.

Breath: The Doorway to Consciousness

Breath is always ready to serve us. But unfortunately we do not have time to listen to it - communicate with it. We are used to it. We are almost forgotten about its existence. We have never thanked it. Each moment, breath is nourishing millions and millions of cells in our body. Breath is our friend. Listen to its language, interpret its words and enter into the mystery of life. Do not control the breath. Just listen to the whisper of your breath. You will find the strength, in the murmur of your breath.

The body, mind, breath, soul and the cosmos are not divided anywhere; they are the one cosmic whole. Breath is the underlying connection between body, mind and soul. Breath is the closest to us. Without breath we cannot survive. The quality of the breath is the quality of our health and mind. When we beautify our breath, we beautify our life. Breathing is your participation with the cosmic dance. When your breath is in harmony, cosmos will nourish you in every sense. Breath is pumping your heart, circulating your blood, and digesting your food. When we sleep at night breath continues and we remain alive and next day we get up and participate in the celebration of life.

Living in the Breath - Use Breath as a Boat

Breath is considered as an anchor. The anchor is often a seaman's last resort in stormy weather. Breath keeps us steady in the storms of uncertainties, and hardship. As an anchor cast into the sand holds a ship securely, so breath, even in the midst of suffering, distress, or sorrow, keeps us firm and grounded. Breath is the boat to cross the ocean of life. Breath is the thread that can bring us back to this moment. Breath is the most wonderful gift of Nature. Be grateful for this wonderful gift. Mindfulness of breath can enable us to live life more fully, more joyously, more attuned to the wonders of life presented by this moment.

Mindfulness is adoration of the beauty of every breath. Only breath keeps the world alive. Mindfulness of breath can cut through the eons of debris collected by the mind. Mindfulness of breath enables us to remove the clutters of negative thoughts and emotions. Beautify your breath – beautify your life.

A Simple Breath Exercise to Free your Mind

Begin your simple mindfulness practice. This simple breath exercise will help you to centre yourself and enhance clarity. Find a quiet place, and then focus your mind on the present moment. Drop for a while whatever you are doing or thinking and start this practice.

1. Gently close your eyes, and take a slow, deep breath, keeping your mouth shut. Focus on breathing out as slowly as possible until your lungs are relatively empty, and mentally count 'one' on your finger. When your lungs

are empty, don't rush to inhale. Pause for a moment and inhale slowly and notice the change from exhalation to inhalation. When your lungs are full, exhale slowly through your nostrils again, and mentally count 'two' on your finger.

2. Notice the breathing process in its entirety. Notice the sensations of your lungs emptying. Notice the feeling of relaxation as the breath goes out. Notice how your shoulders and rib cage are falling as you exhale out. Notice the sensation of air rushing in through your nostrils automatically as your lungs empty themselves out.

3. Repeat the process comfortably up to the count of ten. That is, take ten slow, deep breaths, and focus on exhalation. Let the inhalation happen by itself. If any thoughts come, let them pass by, just as the traffic on the road pass by your car, when you drive, and bring your awareness back to your breathing.

4. After you finish ten breaths, stop counting and breathe normally for a while. You will

notice that your breath has become very slow, deep and subtle. Enjoy your breathing and being in the moment.

5. Open your eyes look around the room and notice what you can see, hear, smell, touch, and feel. Congratulate yourself for completing this exercise. You have been living in the moment, living in the breath.

This simple exercise has the power to free your mind from the emotional clutters of anxiety, worries, depression and repetitive thoughts. You can practice it anytime throughout the day, especially when you find yourself off-center and caught up in repetitive thoughts and feelings.

Compassion –The Mindful Attitude towards Life

Through mindfulness you can know your emotions and respond them with compassion. Mindfulness is refining the art of letting go. Mindfulness is looking at the world with compassionate eyes. Life is a dance. Mindfulness is witnessing that dance.

We can beautify every moment just by changing our attitude towards life. Compassion, love, equanimity, non-attachment, awareness and alertness are the fabrics of inner beauty. As dew drops evaporate in the light of sun, ignorance evaporates in the light of awareness. The journey of compassion starts with the self. Compassion is the attitude to work for the freedom and happiness of everyone. Compassion makes us superior human being with greater understanding. Mindfulness makes us a compassionate human being.

Compassion is all inclusive but you are at the center. Self-love and self-respect is the first step of mindfulness. Love your body, love your mind and love the nature that is around you. Be kind and compassionate towards yourself. Nature has taken millions of years to make you. You are the most precious flower of the nature. You are the most perfect creation of Nature. Take a positive attitude towards your life. You have so many good things. World needs you. World needs your love, attention, talents. Accept yourself as you are. The moment you accept yourself, the entire cosmos is in your help. Learn to be happy with you, what nature has given to you. When you expand the wings of your love, all your limitations will evaporate. You are not alone. You will never be alone. Entire universe is nourishing you, loving you, preparing you and progressing through you. Your experience is the experience of the universe. Learn to be at peace with yourself. You are not like others, you will never be like others and you don't need to be like others. You are the unique beauty of Nature. Identify and appreciate the uniqueness of your life and cultivate that uniqueness of life. Do not compare with others because comparison is meaningless. In front of your uniqueness no one can stand. To cultivate your uniqueness, you need to give something to the world. World needs your unique talent. Focus on the positive side of life. Mindful sharing is moment-to-moment giving something positive to the world. It may be a peaceful thought. It may be a relaxed breathing. It may be just a smiling happy face; it may be your kind look. It may be your love. It may be your attention. It may be your caring. It may be your courage, your strong will power or it may be just happy hugs to near and dear ones. Someone somewhere needs you. Your presence on the earth is an auspicious event of the universe. Mindfulness is accepting and honoring that event moment-to-moment.

However, if you are weak, you may depend on other things like Gods, persons or drugs. When you are too much dependent on others, you are at the mercy of others and suffering follows. But you have the divine spark. It may just need another hard hit to wake you up. Nature gives hard hits to those, who are unaware and too much dependent on others. Because by depending on others, you are denying your Godliness - your greatness. You are denying the power of your Self. Respect yourself, respect others; collaborate and progress.

For loving yourself, you don't need to find any reason. Your existence in this world is enough for that. Just love yourself. Loving yourself is loving the God within you. Develop the faith and trust on yourself. Take charge of your life. If you have faith on yourself miracles will happen to you. There is no greater God in the universe than your love, courage, tranquility and will power. You are your master. You have the master keys to open the locks of your inner world of wisdom and power. Practicing mindfulness is the beginning of unlocking that power.

Part – I

Foundations of Mindfulness

What is Mindfulness?

Mindfulness is a process of relaxed, nonattached, nonreactive, compassionate awareness of the present moment. Life is a dance. Mindfulness is witnessing that dance. Life is a flow of energy. Mindfulness is observing the flow of life from a distance with a curious, attentive and compassionate attitude. It is exploring life with every sense with awareness and kindness. By becoming more aware of our thoughts, feelings, sensations and impulses, we can respond to the situations with choice rather than reacting mechanically.

Mindfulness involves pausing, paying attention, becoming aware of present moment realities, and not being critical about whatever is happening as 'good' or 'bad'. Mindfulness is not a mechanical process. It is a kind, compassionate and caring awareness. Mindfulness is looking at the moment with lenses of compassion. Compassion is being non-critical, being gentle.

When thoughts arise, acknowledge them, let them be; they too have a place in the existence. Don't try to drive them away. Just bring your attention back to the task. Again and again, your attention will wander. As soon as you realize this has happened, gently acknowledge it, note what diverted you, and bring your attention back to the moment, to the task on hand. Mindful eating and mindful walking are the simplest ways to start mindfulness.

Mindfulness makes us creative, compassionate, focused, and loving to ourselves and everyone we encounter. Mindfulness activates our wakefulness and enhances our experience about our deeper inner being. Mindfulness transforms a confused, lonely, guilty, stressed out, lazy, nervous, skeptic person to a inspired, loving, creative, strong, enthusiastic and energetic person.

Mindfulness is not a goal driven step-by-step practice of meditation. It is spacious and relaxed awareness of the present moment. Relaxation and awareness are the two wings of mindfulness. In mindfulness you don't need to follow certain steps or formula. If you follow rigid steps, that will form another habit pattern of mind. In the next chapters we'll discuss many tools and techniques for mindfulness. You can use these techniques for different circumstances.

Adoring the Beauty of Life

Mindfulness is adoring the blessings of the moment that arises and passes by the field of consciousness. If you want peace, adore the blessings of the moment that is given to you. Your breath, your sensations, your feelings, your thoughts and the activities of the nature around you are areas of adoration. Mindfulness is taking in the aroma of life.

Every moment is like a tree. It has flowers and fruits. All flowering trees are not equal. Some are small and some are tall. Some blossom in summer, some are on fall, some are on spring. Every moment has its own fragrance. The flowers attract pollinators, and fruits feed birds and small mammals.

It is adoring the simple moments of life. It may be a simple step, a simple touch, beauty of nature, aroma of food, caring of a pet or a smile of a stranger. Meditation is not repetition or following the unconscious pattern of the mind. It is coming out the unconscious thinking patterns. Meditation is not repetition of the unconscious pattern of the mind. It is coming out of the unconscious patterns.

Mindfulness: An Antidote to Mind-wandering

Mind-wandering originates from the unconscious nature of mind. Researchers tell us that about 47 percent of our waking hours are spent in some form of mind-wandering whether we want to or not. Unlike other animals, we spend a lot of time thinking about the events that happened in the past, might happen in the future, or will never happen at all.

When you are daydreaming or engaged in fantasy, you are most probably thinking unconsciously. These are examples of mind wandering. Unconscious thinking often takes the form of reliving a memory over and over again. It can be a pleasant, often painful past experience, or it can be worrying about the future, as an endless stream of "what ifs". Most of the time unconscious thinking is negative thinking. Entertaining unpleasant thoughts makes people unhappy. Brooding thoughts, obsessive thoughts, worry thoughts, or "what if?" thoughts are the food that unhappiness thrives on. These thoughts fuel anxiety, depression, and other negative mental states. Not surprisingly, mind wandering is the primary cause of unhappiness.

Mind wandering is also the primary cause of anxiety disorders. Often our imaginative worries murder the happiness of the present moment and the beauty of living. Mindfulness is coming out of those unnecessary worries and living a worry free aware life. Inattention, hyperactivity, and impulsivity are associated with increased occurrence of mind-wandering. Mind-wandering is associated with a host of negative consequences including deficits in performance, reduced mood, impaired general intellectual abilities, and disruptions in everyday life experiences. Several scientific studies confirmed that mind-wandering cause unhappiness.

Wandering thoughts are mostly self-related and goal-oriented and the contents of the thoughts are more frequently future-focused than present or past-focused. Some examples of the adverse effects of mind wandering are breaking and spilling things often, clumsiness, and frequent accidents because of carelessness, inattention or thinking about something else.

Too much mind-wandering makes the mind agitated and impure. Scientists noticed that during mind wandering, the default mode network (DMN) of our brain remains active, while the executive or task positive network (TPN) goes to sleep. As a result, too much mind wandering lessens our ability to focus. It can have an adverse effect on our performance, career, and sometimes on our personal safety, when not paying attention to a potentially dangerous task. Inability to pay attention can also adversely affect our relationships.

Life happens in the present – and not the future or the past. Not making a habit of living consciously in the present moment, poses the great risk of missing out on life.

Mindfulness and the Scope for Planning and Creativity

Mindfulness is not a tight rope to bind your creativity, planning, growth and empowerment. Mindfulness does not stop you to take part into the adventures of greater fulfillments and new possibilities of life. Mindfulness does not make you the slave of the present moment but makes you master of the moments. It is the question of how much time we are spending on the anxiety of the past and how much time we are spending on the fantasy of the future. Purpose of mindfulness is to live each moment to the fullest. As we grow older our natural tendency become to stray from the present moment. Our thoughts become dominated by either past memories or future insecurities. When we are obsessed with the future and addicted towards past we will miss the beauty of the present moment.

We can be mindful in our present moment while planning for our future. Our ability to focus our attention on something other than the present is really remarkable. It allows us to learn and plan and reason in ways that no other species of animal can do. We need to recognize our true potential. We need to fulfill our dreams. We need the balance of being and planning. While planning, bring awareness into the planning and know: "I am planning."

Also a certain degree of mind-wandering is associated with enhanced creativity. Normally, peoples remain engaged in demanding tasks or the tasks on hand. During mind-wandering more energy is focused on non-demanding tasks and less on the demanding tasks and performing. This energy devoted to undemanding task during this period often improves creative performance. Day dreaming is bad. It drains away mental energy. Day dreaming is a drug but conscious planning is a medicine.

You can consciously devote a part of your day for creative thinking or creative pursuits. However, by training yourself to remain in the present moment, you train yourself to avoid unconscious thinking. This frees up a great deal of energy, allowing your brain to become more creative and effective once you resume conscious thinking. You will have more mental resource left for planning, creative thinking, and solving problems. It is like by giving your mind a break you are able to tap into the deeper reserve of intelligence within yourself.

Seven Factors of Mindfulness

Mindfulness has seven factors. These seven factors are seven basic requirements of mindfulness. If you understand and apply them, you will improve your mindfulness. Your intention and attitude are very important in the practice of mindfulness. These seven factors are: paying attention to the present moment, non-attached witnessing, gentleness and compassion, patience and relaxation, acceptance and openness, identifying and beautifying the experiences, and becoming spacious and non-reactive. The details of these factors are as follows:

1. Paying attention to the Present moment

Withdraw your thoughts from the past and the future. Focus on the activities and the things that are available in the present moment. Put your energy on observing the present moment activities of the body, mind, and the circumstances. If you are thinking of something else, bring your mind back to the present moment. When your attention wanders, you can bring it back to your breathing, feelings, sensations that arise in your body, or to the activities at your hand. Normally, mind dissipates a big amount of time and energy in wandering to the future, past, and task-unrelated random thoughts. Scientists observed that 47% of the time, we're actually thinking about something other than what we are currently doing. Not surprisingly, the mind wanders mostly in entertaining unpleasant thoughts, obsessive thoughts, brooding thoughts, worrisome thoughts, or "what if?"-thoughts. These are all food for unhappiness. Excessive mind wandering creates stress, strain, anxiety, depression, and other negative mental states. Mindfulness is just opposite to the excessive mind-wandering. Mindfulness is living, loving and appreciating the beauty of life in every moment.

2. Non-attached Witnessing

The second aspect of mindfulness is non-attached witnessing. Do not get emotionally attached to your thoughts, emotions or objects of awareness. The moment you witness something you become separate from it. If you are watching your thoughts, just watch the rush of your thoughts, not interfering, not saying, "This is good. This is bad", not justifying, not appreciating, not blaming. It is non-judgmental witnessing. Your consciousness is just like a mirror. Any thought passes by, the mirror reflects it; that's all. You are not your thoughts. You are the observer of your thoughts.

The intensity of our emotional reaction to external objects reflects the degree of our attachment to them. But the moment you judge something as right or wrong, the mirror becomes clouded.

Through mindfulness, one can develop witnessing, which is a special type of consciousness. Normally, the consciousness exists only as the stream of thoughts. Through mindfulness both the normal thoughts and the witnessing consciousness coexist.

3. Gentleness and Compassion

The third component of mindfulness is a compassionate and kind attitude. Your intention and attitude are very important in the practice of mindfulness. Mindfulness starts with self-compassion – compassion towards your body, mind and soul. Mindfulness and compassion are the key ingredients for a happy, fulfilled and meaningful life. They assist in optimizing your potential both at work and in every aspect of your life. Compassion expands our consciousness. Through expansion and inclusion, we feel relaxed and happy. Compassion works in many levels of our personality. Expansion, joy and freedom are the three elements of compassion. Compassion is the attitude to work for the freedom and happiness of everyone. Compassion is increasing the level of joy of everyone in some way. Compassion is giving something positive to the world. It may be a peaceful thought. It may be a relax breathing. It may be just a smiling happy face; it may be your kind look. It may be your love. It may be your attention. It may be your courage, your strong will power; or it may be just happy hugs to near and dear ones. Somewhere someone needs you. Your presence on the earth is an auspicious event of the universe. Mindfulness is accepting and honoring that event moment-by-moment.

The feeling of friendliness towards happy beings generates an atmosphere of peace and harmony. Empathetic joy is the joy for the happiness for the fellow beings. Cultivate compassion, or deep, genuine sympathy for those beings that are suffering. Mindfulness enables us to understand the deep underline connections with everyone which in turn makes us compassionate.

Compassion enables us to treat everyone with love and respect regardless of race, religion, culture, physical ability and social standards; be it at home, in school, at work or on the streets. It is a journey into the way we think, feel, act and speak about others. Compassion facilitates us in building a deep and wide relationship with everyone on the world. Compassion makes us superior human beings with greater understanding. Even smallest acts of kindness can produces huge impacts in our lives.

Caring about others is primary to our happiness. Helping other people is not only good for them; it's good for us too. It makes us happier and can help to improve our overall well-being.

Research shows that self-compassion is strongly associated with emotional well-being, lower levels of anxiety and depression, and more rewarding personal relationships. Generosity and gratitude are both big contributors to happiness.

Compassion is the key to open the inner locks. For compassion, you don't need to go to the extreme; there are thousand and one scopes within your limits. Compassion is contained in a kind look, a kind touch, a kind word, a kind listening, a kind breath, or a kind thought. Compassion is inviting the healing energy, which heals the suffering of the individual and the society as a whole. Go to the center of your being and from that place spread the energy of your love in every direction.

Sometimes compassion flows like a river, sometimes it falls like heavy rains. When mind is attached, compassion flows like a river – passing only through the soft areas. When mind is free, compassion falls like heavy rains that don't make a difference between hills, dales and meadows. It floods away all difficulties and barriers.

4. Patience and Relaxation

The fourth element of mindfulness is patience and relaxation. Mindfulness is a skill, a habit. It requires time to sprout. Mindfulness grows slowly and gradually. Practice it daily for certain time and allow the things to open up in their own time. For practicing mindfulness, we need to cultivate patience and relaxation. Multi-tasking taxes our brain and it often makes us tense. To become fully present, we need to do one thing at a time. When you are pouring water, just pour water. When you're eating, just eat. When you are taking shower, just do that.

Another necessary point to remember is slow down a little and giving a little extra time in your daily activities. Do them mindfully. Do everything slowly and deliberately. If you are in hurry, you cannot be mindful. Normally, even when we do one task at a time, many of us has a tendency to rush through that task, to finish it. If we do that we, in all probability, will lose our mindfulness. Instead, take your time, and move slowly. Make your actions deliberate, and not rushed or random. It takes practice, but it helps you focus on the task.

Incorporate mindfulness in the things like cleaning the house, washing dishes, or cooking and preparing food. Initially, keep your habit of mindfulness small, but do it consistently, and then gradually increase its span.

With the new technologies of smartphones and the internet, we are constantly bombarded with information. We have persistent temptations to feel constant urgency to talk, to text, to check the mail, check our social network sites, to go and do something else other than attending to the task on hand. One part of our mind is constantly preoccupied with such thoughts. This makes the mind scattered and stressful. We need to learn to do less. We need to just figure out what is really important. If we do less, we can do those things more slowly, more completely and with more concentration. If we stuff our day with many tasks — more than we can gracefully manage, we will be rushing from one thing to the next without stopping to think about what we do. You may think that you are too busy to do less. Actually it is the art of prioritizing things. It's all about the art of managing your schedule wisely so that you always have time to complete each task. Leave some space between things on your schedule. Don't schedule things too close together. Scheduling things too close together will only make you more tense, exhausted and less productive. When you have a more relaxed schedule, you become more creative, more productive.

Mindfulness makes you more productive, more creative.

5. Acceptance and Openness

Do not be over critical about yourself and others. In mindfulness, you need to accept and embrace yourself as you are. Acceptance means bringing more awareness to the object with an open mind, without critical judgment. Letting go of negative thoughts doesn’t mean pushing away the emotions. If you try hard to get rid of some emotions, you may be more attached to them. Bring them to your awareness but do not give them your energy. Acceptance is not the approval of the emotions. Acceptance is coming out of the self-blaming and self-criticizing habits. For example, if you are feeling depressed or angry, here acceptance means observing the flow of emotions from a distance, without trying to change the emotions. Observe the beginning, continuation and the end of the emotions. Experience the emotions as a wave, rising and passing away. You don't necessarily need to act on your emotions. When we approach our emotions with a neutral mindset, we are able to eliminate unwanted reactions. This attitude of acceptance and openness is also helpful in our everyday interactions. When we interact mindfully with a neutral attitude, we eliminate all forms of guess and respond to the situation more appropriately. We find ways to discover depth beyond the surface.

6. Identifying and beautifying the experiences

Every moment has hundreds of negative elements and hundreds of positive elements. Identify the elements and focus on the positives. Initially, you may mentally describe each feelings, sensations or experiences in words. For example you can label the states of your mind, muscles or body parts as "relaxed", "tensed" or "neutral". Similarly, you can label the state of your mind as "thinking", "daydreaming", "analyzing", "remembering", "fantasizing", "worrying", "judging" etc. In the beginning of your practice, labeling the experiences is helpful, but as you progress, put more energy on identifying the raw feelings, sensations and experiences. Notice them as they are, without labeling them. Otherwise, your labeling will keep them alive. When you watch mindfully, but stop labeling the thoughts, they begin to stop. Mindfulness is not labeling the thoughts. It is observing the raw thoughts. If you do too much labeling, you will drop your mindfulness.

The moment you might label a negative thought, accept it and smile to it. Know that it has a reason to exist. Do not drain your energy by being critical. Just take a deep breath, and gracefully shift your attention back to some positive aspect of the moment. Every moment has hundreds of positive elements and hundreds of negative elements. Pay attention to the positive elements.

Every moment comes with some nourishing elements. For example, if you find some worrisome thoughts bothering you, at the same moment you may notice a fragrance in the air. You can gracefully shift your attention to the sweet fragrance. Or, you may ground your attention on the bodily sensation or your breath. A moment soon vanishes into another moment, and new things appear.

A compassionate viewpoint often helps to relax and beautify the moment. Even in the darkest moments there are many hidden stars on the background. Focusing on the stars on background of darkness will beautify your moment. Our stars may be our loved ones like our children, parents, spouse, a loving attendant or a loyal friend. Our stars may be a smile from a stranger, a 'hello' from a neighbor or an inspiring quote from an unknown author. Our stars may be a glass of water, a cup of tea, a deep breath or just a caring touch. It may be hugging a tree, looking at the sky, or just walking on the earth barefoot. In the touch of mindfulness ordinary things become extraordinary. The very fact that we exist here on earth is a miracle. Thousands of events and elements are associated with our existence. Thousand and one things are necessary to maintain our existence. Becoming aware of the miracle of our existence is something that can beautify any moment.

7. Being Spacious and Non-reactive

Another important element in the practice of mindfulness is being careful to not react, but give aware response to a situation. Reaction comes from the unconscious pattern of the mind. Response is the conscious action demanded for the situation.

Being spacious is being open and non-judgmental. Mindfulness helps us become more watchful, less reactive, and more aware of all the motivations — internal-perspectives, beliefs, values, memories and external sight, hearing, smell, taste, touch or bodily sensations — that can impact our behavior in the present moment. To gain empowerment through awareness of all these aspects in the present moment is the key. Otherwise we continue to run on autopilot and feel out of control.

To feel more spacious we need to practice at least five minutes each day doing nothing. We need to learn to just be with ourselves. It is not difficult. It's just a matter of practice. Just sit in silence. Notice the world around you. Become aware of your thoughts. Become comfortable with the silence and stillness. It'll do you a lot of good.

Implementing Mindfulness: Four Small Steps

1. Believe it is possible. The first step for living in mindfulness is believing from the heart that it is possible. Then try mindfulness on a simple activity on hand. Notice what you are doing. For example, if you are eating, notice the color, texture and taste of the food. Take a small step, and make it a success. Appreciate yourself for the achievement. Then, take another step, another... and another...

2. Make mindfulness a priority. Commitment and effort are essential for getting success in mindfulness. If you have trouble fitting mindfulness into your schedule, consider it an important appointment with yourself, and mark it on in your daily agenda. Initially, commit at least a 10-minutes slot twice daily for living in mindfulness. You can practice it while walking, eating or doing your work. Commit to a formal mindfulness meditation schedule for at least 3 or 4 weeks so that it becomes a habit, and try to stick with it.

3. Focus on activities that you enjoy. Never try to make mindfulness a serious affair. Make it a playful and easy task. Do it in a spirit of fun, compassion and commitment. Make it a game you play with yourself. Initially, practice mindfulness more on the happy moments than on the difficult ones. You can start mindfulness while eating or walking.

4. Make mindfulness a social activity. Discussing mindfulness with a friend or loved one or even with your kids will not only make mindfulness more fun and enjoyable; it can also help to motivate you to be more mindful. It'll also make you feel better than practicing alone.

Hierarchy of Mindfulness: Basic Framework of Mindfulness

Mindfulness is a skill that can be cultivated - through practice and determination. The objective of mindfulness is to develop the energy, joy, concentration, tranquility, wisdom and equanimity through compassionate present moment awareness. Mindfulness develops positive qualities such as awareness, insight, wisdom, compassion, and equanimity. With a bit of creativity, you can incorporate mindfulness into any aspect of your life. Practicing mindfulness doesn't need to be a huge commitment — for beginning 5 to 15 minutes each day is good — and even a couple of minutes can be useful.

There are three types of mindfulness "external mindfulness", "internal mindfulness" and "higher mindfulness." External mindfulness is paying attention to the sensory perceptions as they are received by five senses (eyes, ears, nose, tongue, and skin). Internal mindfulness includes awareness about bodily functions, feelings, sensations, thoughts, internal-perspectives, beliefs, values, and memories. Higher mindfulness is awareness about the higher being, the ultimate reality.

Table 1 shows ten types of awareness according to their depth and subtlety. Image – 1 shows the hierarchy of mindfulness. It has five levels of awareness. You can start from the external awareness and move towards the top. However, there is no specific formula; you can start from any place.

Table – 1: Types of Awareness

Mindfulness	Awareness Types
External Mindfulness	1. Environmental awareness
	2. Activity awareness
Internal Mindfulness	3. Posture awareness
	4. Body parts awareness
	5. Breathing awareness
	6. Body sensation awareness
	7. Feelings awareness
	8. Thought awareness
	9. Awareness of mental states
Higher Mindfulness	10. Awareness of factors of awakening
	11. Awareness of the being
	12. Awareness of the Ultimate Essence

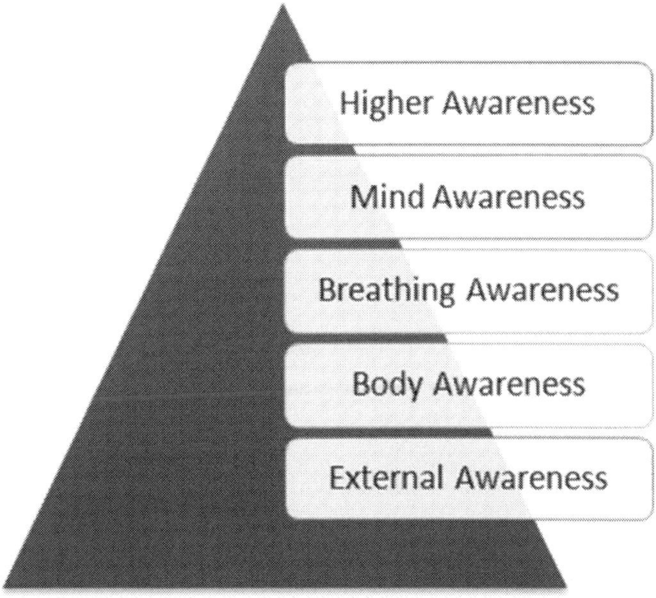

Image – 1: Hierarchy of mindfulness

1. External Environmental Awareness:

Environmental awareness is developing mindfulness about the surroundings. It is awareness about the things that you are seeing, hearing, smelling, tasting and touching.

Visual awareness

Visual awareness deals with the objects that you are seeing in the present moment. There are lots of things to see in the present moment. You can see birds on the tree, flying insects in the air or just the beauty of the roof, walls and the floor. You can see the jumps of the frogs in the meadow behind the old pines. Notice the objects that are in front of you, above the head, below the feet and on the sides. Focus on any one of them and notice the characteristics of the object without judgment or attachment. Notice the colors, textures, forms and the sizes of the objects. The object may be a wall, a table, a chair, a computer, a person, a car, a tree, a house, or any other things. Notice it, as it is, without judgment or interpretation of good or bad. Look at the objects with great care and full attention. Notice the dark spots, and colors of shade. Notice the raw sensations of the scenes, without labeling them.

Sound awareness

Pay attention to the sounds that reach your ear. Without searching for sounds, let them come to you and fill your ears. You may pick up individual sounds. You might recognize a friendly voice, a bird's note, a siren in the distance, an aircraft overhead, or music coming from your neighbor's house. It might be the sound of your breath as it moves through your nostrils. The list is endless. Notice the nature of the sound. Is it sharp or mellow, broken or continuous, long or short? Notice the variations in the sound. Some are relatively long and some are just brief notes. Some sounds come from nearby and some seem to come from far away. You may notice the volume, tone, pitch, pattern and duration of the sounds. Try to notice them without mental interpretation or analysis of good or bad. Notice the silence in between the sounds. Notice the network of thoughts that arise as you listen to the sounds.

Smell awareness

When you go out to the nature, take a deep breath of the fresh air. You can notice the fragrance of the fallen leaves, damp earth, and sweet flowers. Everywhere, there is some smell. Normally, we do not notice them at all. Smell awareness starts with the questions like: What is the smell entering into my nose? Is it pleasant, unpleasant or neutral? Is it a smell of food, flower, perfume, chemical, smoke, or something else? You repeat the questions, and the answers will ground you to the present moment. Each smell may activate a network of associations. Observe those associations. For example the smell of freshly baked breads may stir some childhood memories like the memory of your grandma baking breads for you. Whenever you notice some smells, also notice what those smells do to you. Some smell may depress you. Some smell may elate or inspire you. Notice those feelings too.

Taste awareness

We have an average of 10,000 taste buds, predominantly on the tongue, but they are also positioned on the roof of the mouth and near the pharynx. Taste and smell together give us the sensory impression of a flavor. Taste is categorized in to five basic categories: sweet, bitter, sour, salty and pungent. Notice the taste in your tongue, when you take some food. Are they sweet, sour, bitter, salty or pungent? Examine how your body responds to sweet, bitter, sour, salty and pungent tastes. Does your breathing change? Does a certain taste relax or tense you?

Touch awareness

Touch is the first sense in humans that develops in the womb of mother. The sense of touch continuously informs the brain about the status of different areas of the body. We can never voluntarily shut down our sense of touch. The sense of touch, commonly consist of pressure, temperature, pleasure, pain, muscle tension or relaxation, and movement. You can feel the touch of clothes, air, person, water or any other things. Pay attention to those touches. Are they pleasant, unpleasant or neutral? Examine how your mind responds to the touches. Are you relaxed or tensed, when you feel a certain touch?

2. Activity Awareness

It is mindfulness about the activities that you are doing or activities that are going on in your presence in the present moment. Pay attention to what you are doing. Are you eating, drinking, reading, feeling sleepy, daydreaming, writing, walking or talking?

Mentally make a note of the activities that you are doing in the present moment.

3. Body Posture Awareness

Posture awareness is the easiest way to live in the present moment. Throughout the day we change our postures. We are walking, standing, sitting or lying down. We continuously change the positions of our body parts. We do this sometimes consciously, but most often unconsciously. Mindfulness of posture is development of the non-judgmental awareness of the body-postures during sitting, standing, walking, and lying down. Examine the position of your body. Is it walking, standing, sitting or in lying down position? Notice how the body is changing its positions. Notice if the body is bending, straightening or stretching.

Whether it is sitting at your desk writing or typing at the keyboard, once you become aware of your posture, the body will automatically try to adjust its position form a bad posture to a good one. As you perform mindfulness repeatedly, your nervous system will start to adapt to the new position. On the other hand, if you do not notice your posture, you create poor postural habits on a daily basis that most of the people don't even realize they are doing but it eventually contribute to physical pain in the future. Repetitive poor posture day after day, year after year will give you trouble sooner or later.

4. Body Parts Awareness

It is noticing the positions of the body parts like arms, legs, ears, head, shoulders, elbows, hips, knuckles, spine and feet. It is observing the changing nature of the positions of the body parts. This type of mindfulness is part of posture awareness. It is noticing the rising and falling nature of the body postures. Examine how all the body parts are changing their positions every time. Developing awareness about the body parts throughout the day trains the mind to know the unconscious habit patterns of the body.

5. Breathing Awareness

Only breath keeps the world alive. Adore the beauty of every breath. You can focus on any part of the breath, or area of the breathing process that feels most prominent for you. It may be where the air comes in and out of your nostrils, or the way the abdomen rises and falls with each breath. Historically, Buddha explained this practice as – "as you breathe in, know that you are breathing in; and, as you breathe out, know that you are breathing out." No analysis of "good" or "bad". Your aim is not to control the breathing process but just to observe it. Your aim is to watch and follow the phenomena, the processes concerned with the breathing in and breathing out. No grasping. The moment you start observing the phenomena, you consciousness will change. Mental clouds will disappear. Gradually your mind will be calm and quite.

Make no effort to change the rhythm of your breathing. In the beginning, it is often difficult to maintain the awareness of the breathing. Mental chattering and other thoughts may interfere with your breathing awareness. No matter whatever the thought arises, bring the awareness back on your breathing. As soon as a thought crosses your mind, just notice it, and let it go, without following it.

6. Body sensation awareness

Notice the tension spots throughout your body. Feel the sensations in various body parts. You can start from your head and continue with your shoulders, arms, chest, belly, hips, upper legs, lower legs, and feet. Observe the sensations from head to toe and toe to head. Body sensations include heat, warmth, cold, pain, numbness, itching, tingling, lightness, heaviness, hardness and softness. Sensations have various physical elements: the earth element (hardness, softness, heaviness, lightness or numbness), the air element (wave like vibrations), fire element (heat, cold, warmth, itching or tingling) and the water element (rigidity, circulation and fluidity). Take any body parts or body area and notice the sensations. Notice whether it is painful, pleasant or neutral.

7. Feelings awareness

There are two types of feelings; positive feelings and negative feelings. Happy, confidence, joy, bravery, etc. are positive feelings. Depression, fear, sadness, anxiety, anger, jealousy, hatred, fear, hurt and other painful emotions are negative feelings. The skill of equanimity depends upon the ability to detach yourself from the feelings. In mindfulness just observe the feelings without any judgment, attachment or aversion. Experience the feelings now and here with a gentle non-judgmental and compassionate way. Remind yourself that you are not your feelings. You are the observer of your feelings. Remain focused on the feelings, and not with the associated thoughts.

8. Thought awareness

Your thoughts are of the nature of an inner dialogue. You have an average of about six thousand thoughts a day, most of which are repetitive and come from a habitual pattern. Thought awareness is critical because thoughts trigger emotions. A thought may be an idea, an image, a sound, a memory, a fantasy or even an emotional feeling that arises within you. Thought awareness is the process by which you observe your thoughts in the present moment without attachment or aversion. Notice the thoughts as a flow; that are arising, persisting, and then passing away in your mind. You can imagine your mind as a vast open sky, and thoughts are simply like clouds of different colors, passing through the open space. There may be negative thoughts that carry worries, fear and self-criticism. There may be positive thoughts carrying joy, happiness and confidence. Just notice them. Remind yourself that you are not your thoughts. You are the observer of the thoughts.

You may be caught up in your thoughts instead of observing them. As soon as you realize that, gently and compassionately return to observing the thoughts. Try to observe your thoughts without getting involved into the content of the thoughts. Your thoughts are just thoughts – you are the master and they are your servants.

Let your internal eye sweep across the inner sky. You may lie down in the grass and browse through the fluffy clouds of the mind. They may look like animals, cities or gates to the heaven. Just notice them. If you look for an extensive period of time you will see a continual change. There is neither beginning nor end. Clouds and clarity are not always in balance. Only the form and colors of the cloud changes and the sky remain changeless. Focus your energy on that changeless inner sky.

9. Awareness of mental states

Investigate the current state of your mind. There are three basic mental states; positive, negative and neutral. Again, each of them can be divided into sub groups. The positive mental states can be classified as relaxed mind, clear mind, happy mind, compassionate mind, wisdom mind and calm or tranquil mind. The negative mental states are roaming mind, chattering mind, tired mind, dull mind, clouded or confused mind, lazy mind, emotional mind, angry mind, jealous mind, forgetful mind, tensed mind and unhappy mind. Just notice the state of your mind. Do not get caught up with the content of the mind. Observe the state of the mind from a distance. Notice the arising and passing away of the mental states.

Higher Levels of Mindfulness

As you intensify the mindfulness on mental states, the contents of the mind will become increasingly refined. After some time, it will appear that there is an observer behind the mental processes. This observer mind is much above the mental states. However, as you intensify your practice of observing the mind, the feeling of a separate observer will disappear. You will find that there is no solid self as the observer. There is only the observation. You will find as if, the objects of mind are coming from nowhere and vanishing into nowhere.

10. Awakening factor awareness

The next stage is mindfulness about the awakening factors. This is a subtler level of awareness. It is awareness about the very journey of mindfulness. At this level your mindfulness becomes extremely subtle and it can know any object or mental state much before it sprouts in your mind. The factors of awakening are energy, rapture, tranquility, concentration and equanimity. In the journey of mindfulness you gradually become aware of these higher states of awakening. Notice how these factors arise and pass away. Attachment or clinging to any of these factors will only bring dissatisfaction. Notice how these factors are closely interlinked.

11. Awareness of the being

In the final stage of mindfulness, you turn the light of mindfulness within, towards the observer itself. It is then that you realize that the notion of the individual self is not a reality. Only the pure awareness of being exists. At this stage deep feeling of compassion arises towards all beings of the existence. You realize that everything and being are deeply interconnected. You find yourself in this huge expanse of empty space. It is your infinite inner being. You find that all forms, sights, sounds, smell, touch, taste are like objectless empty space. But still there exists a fine line between the feeler and the infinite space. This awareness is free from all identifications. In the expanded awareness of the being, you are like the sky, it is always present, and you are living in it all the time. It is not fantasy, fiction or imagination. It is the reality.

12. Awareness of the Ultimate

In the final state of being, awareness is completely empty of thoughts and objects, so there is nothing to observe; nor is there any observer. There is no individual self that used to observe. You transcend the ordinary perception of the seer, seen and seeing. The concept of object and subject vanishes. Only the awareness of profound oneness exists. This is the state of profound inner and outer harmony. At this state there is cessation of becoming and cessation of repetitive cycle of birth and death.

This experience of absolute organic unity of your consciousness has been called by different names - nirvana, moksha, liberation, enlightenment, or illumination. This is the ultimate peak; this is the ultimate goal of human life.

Part II

Mindfulness of Daily Activities

Practicing mindfulness during daily routine activities can beautify your day and enliven your life. Moving on autopilot through our daily activities can make life seem dull and boring. To break away from this, try bringing awareness to the daily activities that you normally do on autopilot. Any task that you perform on a daily basis can be a practice of mindfulness. For example, walking, eating, opening the door, drinking a cup of tea, washing the dishes, driving a car — each can be an exercise in mindfulness. It becomes a mindfulness practice when you decide to perform the task with your full attention and be completely present in the moment. Try to notice what is going on around you, in your body, and in your mind, as you do your daily activities, rather than thinking about something else. For instance, you can pay more attention as you are brushing your teeth, taking a shower, eating your breakfast, driving your car or walking to work.

You can pay attention to your bodily movements while standing, walking, or talking to people. Mindfulness is not about changing anything you notice – it's just about noticing what is actually going on during your everyday task. It doesn't matter if your mind wanders thousand times from what you are sensing and feeling in your body, as you do your task; just gently bring your attention back to your task. Practice paying attention to every detail of the task, and when thoughts come up, instead of thinking about how annoying they are, acknowledge them, and refocus your attention on your activity. Being present here and now is the only way to enjoy your life to the fullest. Being mindful enhances your enjoyment of your food, your work, and your friends and family.

In this section we'll discuss twelve mindfulness practices for daily activities. You can use these practices in your daily life.

1. Waking up in Mindfulness

You may often wake up feeling anxious or stressed. It's especially common for those with stressful jobs. Generally, morning anxiety occurs if you go to bed too late, watching challenging TV programs before your sleep, having high workload or too many clutters and electronic items in your bedroom like phones, tablet, and laptop. On waking, the body tenses and jumps into 'fight or flight' response at the memory and anticipation of another stress-filled day ahead. Thus a session of negative thinking ensues before the day has even begun, and a repeating cycle of early morning anxiety is created. On waking up, our bodies generate a hormone called cortisol. It is released to increase our alertness, and as a result the sleep hormone melatonin is decreased. However, cortisol is also released as a response to stress, and as a result, it can make us feel tense and anxious, if we are exposed to chronic stress. Avoid the temptation to stay in bed with negative thoughts. Fill your mind with positive thoughts. Positive self-talk can transform your life.

What is the first thing you do when you get out of bed each morning? If you check phone, or emails, you are not alone. Many people start their day by checking their phones and emails. Instead of checking office emails or the notifications of your social media profiles, take out some time for being with yourself and plan out your whole day in a systematic way.

With morning mindfulness you can start your day fresh and happy. Mindfulness practice in the morning after you wake up helps to tone up your nervous system for the rest of the day. When you wake up, listen to your own breath, your own inner voice, your own wisdom. This is another beautiful day, and another opportunity to grow. Don't jump into the daily activities like email checking or coffee making immediately after waking up.

- Sit quietly for a few moments, and notice the morning silence and the sounds in the environment.
- Notice how your eyes feel — are they tired or relaxed? Are you squinting? Do you perceive fatigue in the muscles around your eyes? Don't try to do anything with your eyes – simply notice whatever is there; pay attention to it, and be aware of it.

- Pay attention to your breath, as they flow in and out regularly one after the other. This will ground you in the present moment and help you to move into a state of awareness and calmness. Don't try to do anything with your breathing – simply notice it, pay attention to it and be aware of it.

- Listen to the fascinating notes of the birds, if you happen to live close to Nature. Notice the variations in the sound. Some are relatively long and some are just brief calls. Notice them.

- Pay attention to what is happening right now. Observe the Nature, the green trees, and the morning Sun.

2. Mindful Tooth Brushing

Tooth Brushing is a seemingly simple activity, but it is one of the easiest ways to put mindfulness into practice, and understand the concept of mindfulness. While brushing our teeth our mind often wonders. We may be thinking and planning for something else — it may be about going to work, visiting family and friends or simply running for the workplace.

Be aware of the activities that you are doing in present moment, and you'll find that your tooth brushing is even more enjoyable than usual—and you can take satisfaction in knowing that you're developing mindfulness at the same time! Try brushing mindfully.

- Pay attention to what is happening right now. As you hold the toothbrush on your hand, feel the touch of it. Notice the color of the toothbrush, shape and sizes of the brush bristles. As you put toothpaste on the brush, observe the color; notice the smell of the paste.
- How do the brush and the paste feel and taste? Is it rough or smooth, enjoyable, or something else? Does it taste minty, pungent, sweet or something else?
- Notice what the bristles feel like while you're brushing the front, top, and back

of your teeth and how it feels to brush your gums and your tongue.

- Pay attention to your breath. Is it deep or shallow, easy or strained? Do not try to change it.
- Observe the muscles you are using. Notice what your other hand is doing.
- Notice the state of your mind. Is it thinking, planning, remembering, imagining or daydreaming? If you are lost in thought, gently bring the attention back to the sensations of brushing the teeth here and now.
- Inspect the movement of your body while you brush. Notice the movements of your lips, tongue, wrist and the arm.
- As you are washing, examine the sensations in your mouth. What temperature is the water? Is it chilly, cool, warm or slightly warm? Notice the sound of the water as you rinse your mouth and face. How does your mouth

feel? Is it cool, fresh, refreshed or something else?

The purpose is to keep the mind in the present moment and to brush the teeth while being aware of and paying attention to thoughts, physical sensations and emotions that occurred during the brushing.

3. Taking the Shower Mindfully

Stress consumes and reduces your energy. If you are feeling lethargic and tired despite getting enough sleep, it may be your stress pulling you down. A nice mindful shower may be just what you need to feel alive and ready to start your day.

Your morning shower is a great place to practice mindfulness. Taking shower can help you feel fresh and revitalized. You can get much more than just cleaning. Usually we do not notice the activities during showering. Showering is so habitual a process that you will initially find it very difficult to observe the steps of showering activities. However, if you slow down the process, it will be easier for you to notice the activities. Break this habit and try showering mindfully and enjoy the aliveness of the water.

By taking a mindful shower, you will feel better, both physically and emotionally. The sweet smells of shampoos, conditioners, and soaps can help to reduce your stress levels too. Showers have the power to wake up you, both physically and mentally.

- Enter into your personal shower and pause for a moment. Take notice of your body posture and feel the sensations from your head to toes.

- Feel the temperature of the water as you turn on the shower. Notice feeling as water touches the body. Is it chilly, cool, warm or slightly warm? Discover the aliveness of the water, and the relaxing effects of the sensation as it touches your body. Water has special powers in erasing the stress and rejuvenating our body. As it touches the skin and muscles, it calms the organs and endocrine system by stimulating nerve reflexes on various parts of the body. Notice how the water in motion stimulates the touch receptors on the skin. How does it feel as it is gently releasing the tensed muscles? Notice the sounds of the water as you rinse your body and face. How does your body feel? Is it cool, fresh, refreshed or something else?

- Observe the movements of your hands, when you use shampoo, soap, scrub or gel. Notice the scents of the soaps and shampoo, and the feel of them against your skin.

- Feel the touch sensations as you rub the body with your hands. Your mind may drifts away from showering, gently refocus on showering.

- Notice the scene of the water droplets on the walls or shower screen, the water droplets going down your body and the steam rising upwards.

- Observe any other sensations or changes in your body as you shower. How are you breathing? Can you hear yourself breathing? Notice your body temperature— do you feel comfortable?

- Most importantly, enjoy the showering activity. The shower is a wonderful opportunity to be present and awake.

When thoughts arise, acknowledge them, let them be, and gently bring your attention back to the shower. Forget all the worries for these 15 minutes. Feel the rejuvenating power of the water, soaps and the scents. Escape from the world and all of its worries to enliven you.

4. Mindful Breathing

Breathing is something we all do. Our body knows how to do this. It is a natural physiological activity that is regulated by the human brain to exchange oxygen and carbon dioxide with the air outside. However, the breathing motion or rhythm is not constant. It changes in association to different physical and emotional states, such as speaking, singing, walking, working or, feeling fear, stress, anxiety, etc. Chest breathing is human's natural response to emergencies. When people feel stressed or anxious, they tend to increase the breathing rate and shift from diaphragmatic breathing to chest breathing, in order to take in extra oxygen to defend themselves. However, stressful breathing breaks the natural rhythm and disturbs the balance between oxygen and carbon dioxide in the body, which leads to a variety of health problems. Mindful breathing is an antidote for stressful breathing and stressful living.

Breathing awareness is the most fundamental to mindfulness practice. Mindful breathing will help you to gain mastery over stress. By learning mindfulness of breathing you can reduce or eliminate stress from your body and mind. You can practice mindful breathing anytime throughout the day. It is easy, simple and most effective way for calming the mind. It will help you to produce a sense of power and mastery, thereby reducing anxiety and restoring a sense of calm.

You can focus on any area of the breath that feels most prominent for you. It may be where the air comes in and leaves your nostrils; it may be the way the abdomen rises and falls with each breath. Historically, Buddha explained this practice as – “as you breathe in, know that you are breathing in; and, as you breathe out, know that you are breathing out." No analysis of "good" or "bad". Your aim is not to control the breathing process but just to observe it. Your aim is to watch and follow the phenomenon, the processes, concerned with breathing in and breathing out. No grasping is necessary. Just pure awareness of the process is all that is needed. The moment you start observing the phenomena, you consciousness will change. A silence, a beauty will arise on its own. Gradually your mind will be calm and quite.

Make no effort to change the rhythm of your breathing. In the beginning, it is often difficult to maintain the awareness of the breathing. Mental chattering and other thoughts may interfere with your breathing awareness. No matter whatever thoughts arise, bring your attention back to the awareness of the breathing. As soon as a thought crosses your mind, just notice it, and let it go, without following it.

5. Mindful Driving

Driving is a complex task, requiring full concentration and a calm attitude. Heightened emotions such as stress, anger, resentment or restlessness are cognitive distractions that can significantly impede drivers' ability to spot and respond to hazards. Your state of mind is a vital element in safe driving. To drive safely you should be calm, relaxed and alert. Losing the attention, and allowing the mind to wander, is quite a common daily occurrence. This happens in all ages and to all people. This often occurs, when you are bored, tired, or doing something you don't like doing. It may happen if you are driving every day in the same known route. Losing your attention could be risky, if you are driving. Mindful driving will help you become more focused, relaxed, and successful once you get to your destination.

While driving, safety is the first priority. For that you need hundred percent of your attention given to the present moment activities that are going around. Car driving in a busy city area requires more attention than a freeway driving. Hence, first, you can practice mindful driving in freeway and then you can practice it in the city area. In city driving, you need more mindfulness about the road, traffic signals and the movements of the other vehicles. Car driving under the influence of mind wandering is always dangerous. Instead of thinking something else, pay attention to the driving. Mindful driving, in fact, is the safest way to drive. The purpose is that every time the mind wanders, you bring yourself back to the present moment driving experience.

The Practice:

- Buckle up and sit comfortably on the seat. Before you start the engine, become aware of your body. Experience the feelings on your hands on the steering wheel, the touch of your body on the seat, and your foot on the pedal.

- Start to drive and notice the environment as you drive: through your windshield, and on your mirrors. Mentally note the colors and shapes of the road, other cars and the surroundings without unnecessary analysis of what you are seeing.

- Notice the sounds you hear – the noises of your car, the sounds made by other cars, and the murmur and buzz of the world around you without analyzing too much of what you are hearing.

- Obviously, when you're driving it is not recommended that you close your eyes and focus on your breathing. Off course you do not do that. Pay full attention on the road and to the driving activities. Keep your normal alertness active. Keep a constant awareness about the surroundings. Maintain awareness about three things: what you see on the road, what you hear and your body feelings. You need primary mindfulness about the road, traffic signals and the movements of the other vehicles.

- Become aware of when you are slowing down or speeding up, and changing the gear. Notice the quality of your driving. Are you driving too fast, too slow or normal? Do not judge it as "good" or 'bad." Just notice it.

- Your main focus will be your task, driving, but sometimes you can try to keep your awareness about your body. Are you sitting erect or bent over? Are you in the present moment, or are you getting out ahead of yourself and thinking something else?

- When you are stopped at a red light or in a traffic jam, you can pay attention to other people, sky, trees, or quality of your mind. You can monitor your bodily sensations. Is there tension in your shoulders, face, hands, or back? Become aware of body tension. Are your hands wrapped tightly around the steering wheel? Are your stomach too tight and shoulders raised? Make yourself comfortable.

- If you are used to keep radio, a book on tape, or a podcast on, it is normally not recommended in mindful driving. However, if you must listen to something while you drive, keep in mind that your primary focus is driving and the road ahead. What you are listening to are secondary and should not distract you from the driving. If your mind wanders, take a breath and gently bring your attention back to the road ahead, your body on the seat, hands on the steering wheel and feet on the pedal.

- Observe the muscles that you are using in driving. Notice what your hands are doing. Notice the state of your mind. Is it thinking, planning, remembering, imagining or daydreaming? If you are lost in thought, gently bring the attention back to the driving experience here and now.

- Mindful driving can facilitate a better relationship with other road users. Don't get upset by behavior of other road users. Notice your attitude and the attitudes of the other road users. Make a practice of noticing other cars trying to enter the road, and adjust your speed so that you can let them out, if it's safe to do so.

- Notice the level of relaxation, anxiety, tension or agitation in your mind. Try to enjoy your drive. Worrying is not going to help you. No point in blaming the road conditions or other road users. Once you have set off on your way, committing to driving with awareness and kindness to others is the best thing you can do.

6. Mindfulness at Office

No matter what type of job you are involved in, it is not uncommon to experience increased mental pressure during the beginning of the workday. After all, there may be a long list of tasks to be done, deadlines to be met, and challenging priorities demanding your immediate attention. Workload in the office can overwhelm anybody. You need to be thoughtful and discriminative enough to prioritize your tasks, attending them one by one. Instead of feeling overwhelmed by the amount of work you need to complete by the end of the day, and rushing from one to another, consider to integrate a more deliberate, calm, and mindful approach for boosting focus at work. Being mindful at your work will take the pressure out of you, boost your focus and increase your productivity.

Office is the ideal place for practicing mindfulness. Mindfulness can help you to reduce stress, anxiety and conflict, and increase spirit, efficiency and emotional intelligence.

No matter how rushed your morning hours at your jobs may feel, make use of brief moments to practice mindfulness, like taking 10 seconds to take a few slow, deep breaths as you move from one activity to the next.

Mindfulness can also improve your communication skill in the office. Through mindfulness, you can become aware about your emotions as they arise, which gives you many choices to handle them. Mindfulness will help you to deal with stressful situations with more ease, comfort, and grace. To practice mindfulness, you will do your work mindfully, and at the same time, you'll observe yourself. From time to time you will be keeping a note of your body posture, breathing quality or the emotional states of your mind. Work, mindfulness, gratitude and compassion must go together for greater efficiency at job.

The Practice

Get organized

Starting your morning in a quiet mind will help you become more effective throughout the day. Mindfully plan your activities before you begin your workday. Break your main tasks into small sub-tasks. Pay attention to prioritizing what you need to do. Integrate small spaces between the tasks. Write down your to-do list on a paper. Mindfully prepare your to-do list by focusing on those projects that will have the most impact and are best aligned with your goals. This will keep you focused, reduce your scattering thoughts and wastage of mental energies. If you are not planning your time, you are unknowingly planning to be stressed. Mindfully identify your main time thieves. What do you do that sucks up your time? Once you make the list, stop re-thinking, re-estimating and rewriting it. Just focus on your immediate goals that will help you to accomplish the big goal.

Do one thing at a time

Work on one thing at a time. No one gets better results by doing several tasks simultaneously. Pay each task full attention that it deserves, and when it's complete, tick it off the list. While doing your activities, if your mind wanders into planning, daydream, or criticism, notice where it has gone and gently bring it back to the present moment.

Micro-mindfulness

At office micro-mindfulness is very helpful. Micro-mindfulness is a small period of awareness that you can integrate into your daily activities. It can be done in many ways.

Pause for a moment. Pay attention to what your fingers or hands are doing. Sense the tingling in your hands. Take a note of the positions of your body parts - your legs, hands or head. Feel the test in your mouth or feel the air in your nose. Then go back to your work.

You may practice micro-mindfulness at job by pausing to take a few deep breaths before checking emails.

You may practice micro-mindfulness at job, by taking a very small break once in a while, leaving the desk and going for a brisk walk. Just take a few deep breaths and pay attention to the environment, while walking.

Practice of micro-mindfulness is very important when you feel stressed. Sit up straight and take five deep breaths, noticing the comforting sensation of inhalation and the feeling of release during exhalation.

Take regular breaks

Try to take 1 – 3 minutes breaks per hour. This is a great chance to check your posture and breathing, to have a brisk walk or exercise your body. When you breathe, turn away from the computer screen, close your eyes and exhale fully. Sense the breath moving in and out; see what you notice about the air you take in and expel. Walking around frequently increases blood circulation throughout your body giving you more energy. If you cannot leave your desk, you can do a few mindful stretching exercises right in your chair or you can just stand up for a few minutes and feel the tensions in the body parts.

Master your mindset

In your office, how you deal with pressure is important for your efficiency and success. If you can master your mindset, you can master your success. Pay attention to your emotions. Sometimes, you may be feeling frustrated or angry. This may generate agitated feeling in your body, which may cause you to react. In that situation, take a deep breath first and reflect on what's behind your anger. Anger-driven actions almost always do more harm than good, to you and others alike. The way you think leads to your feelings, and that dictates your actions. Give a pause before you reply. A more measured response is usually better than a snap reaction. If you are feeling stressed, scared, or fearful, just accept these thoughts mindfully. Notice them mindfully and take a few deep breaths. They will dissolve.

Remember, what you focus on expands. Focus on positive things.

Mindful Conversations

Good communication is essential for success in career as well as relationships. Conversation is a two-way flow of listening and speaking. You must master the art of mindful listening and speaking. For that you need to give sufficient time.

Be present and carefully listen to what other person is saying. Give them your full attention. It is more important at least during the first two or three minutes of any conversation. Without judgment, with innocence and openness, pay close attention to their voice, their body language, and even the tone of their words. Be mindful, and practice looking at the other person's eye during the conversation. Focus more intently on the present moment with a sense of sincerity and candidness.

Then respond by reflecting on what they said so that they know you understand. We frequently only interpret our version of what the other person said. Also, take a note of your own mind and emotions during the conversation. How did you feel? Did you feel acknowledged, appreciated, and accepted? If yes, give genuine “thank you”. If not, notice your own feelings.

Practice speaking mindfully and become more aware of what you want to say. Mindfully choose your words to get your ideas across. Do not speak out of reaction. In mindful interaction, it is important to avoid hurtful words. Become mindful of keeping your value or dignity intact in any situation. In a difficult situation, internal negativity may develop stress but mindfulness makes you able to hold your reaction. Instead of immediately reacting, pay attention to the sensations of your body. Feel your feet on the floor or feel your breath. Give yourself an extra second or two to process what has just been said to you. This will give you some extra space to gather yourself, collect your thoughts and then confidently give appropriate response.

Notice the speed at which you are speaking. Is it fast, slow or normal? Mostly people speak fast. They believe that by rushing to say everything, they will keep the listener's attention. This is not so. In fact, talking fast is difficult to understand, distracting, and will quickly bore the listener. Similarly do not speak too slowly. Speaking mindfully at a medium speed, with deliberate choice of words, you can win the respect and attention of your listener.

Articulate your words clearly and fully. Take your time to speak with purpose. Don't rush to respond. Give yourself an extra second or two to process what you listen. Rushing to utter words may make you seem anxious and like you're trying too hard.

Notice how you are giving pauses. Give pause effectively. Notice pauses not only at the end of sentences, but in the middle of them as well. Notice where you can and should wait for an extra second. Especially with stories, this builds suspense and engages the listener.

Notice the nature of your voice. Is it monotonous or passionate? Be mindful to speak with passion and purpose. Do not speak in a monotonous voice. That will put people to sleep. Emphasize words in your sentences to reflect your emotions. Notice your hand gestures and facial expressions during conversation. Are you over acting, under acting or normal? If you're passionate about what you say, your audience will be passionate about it, too. Being mindful about how you speak will especially come useful when you need to give a speech or a demonstration. It will also improve your relation with your co-workers. Good communication is essential to any healthy relationship.

Mindfulness in sitting posture

Mindfulness of posture is vital. Pay attention to your posture more. Cultivate healthier postural habits. At work, many of us need to sit at our desks and stare at the computer screen for hours. Studies found that regular sitting for long periods of time at work, takes years off from the life. The human body has evolved to and is biologically designed to be mobile, and not sedentary. Research tells us that anyone sitting more than 6 hours a day amplifies risk of health problems and this much sitting may be as bad as smoking a pack of cigarettes every day.

When you sit on a chair, your lower back or the lumbar region of your spinal cord should get optimum support. This would help maintain a good posture and save you from lower back ache in the long run. Try to keep the top of the screen at an eye level. Make sure that both the arms and the wrists are properly supported by the chair and the table, while the head is resting back on the chair.

Practice balanced sitting. Notice the body parts where the weight is imbalanced. Notice what's uncomfortable. Maintain the natural curve of your spine. Are you working in the same posture? Make sure to change your position throughout the day.

Mindful lunch break

Take your lunch break away from you desk. When we get outside in nature our stress and depression is reduced, and we increase our energy, productivity and creativity. You may go to lunch with co-workers. When you go to a restaurant, as you walk or drive to the restaurant, enjoy your conversation, laughter and sharing. Taste your food. Pay full attention to what you're doing, eating, or drinking. You may choose to eat one lunch every week in silence. Use this as a time to eat slowly and be with yourself.

Mindfulness at the end of the day

When you've finished your desk work for the day, take 2-3 minutes to review what you have done. Acknowledge and congratulate yourself for what you’ve accomplished. Let go of the things that did not go well. Make a list for tomorrow. Stand up and stretch. Breathe fully in and out and allow your work to melt away into the past and bring yourself fully back into the present moment. As you are leaving work, bring your awareness to walking. Pay attention to the outside world. Mindfully see the trees and open sky. Listen to the sounds outside of your workplace.

7. Mindful De-cluttering

Clutters are the luggage of the past that are not useful, but sucks energy and space. There are three types of clutter physical, mental and digital. Clutter is anything that you have accumulated but not useful. You keep them because of your unawareness, emotional attachments or believe that they will come useful one day. Clutter takes our time, energy or space, and destroys our serenity.

Clutter can be any things like old books, outgrown clothes, obsolete papers, broken toys, disliked gifts, meaningless activity, old bitterness, or unsatisfying relationships. Digital clutter includes things like old software, junk emails, unused videos, old music and documents files.

Even if there are little bits of messes all around us, they quietly suck our energy. It may be several extra items on the kitchen counter, a few extra bottles of this and that around the tub, some old magazines and books strewn around like they were tossed, or a few old garments in your wardrobe that you neither use any more nor can you dispose them. Though, taken individually, they don't seem like much, but overall they add to the clutters in your house and in your life. When we have a tidy space around us, our mind is free to relax rather than subconsciously being continuously engaged in processing what is in front of it.

Mental clutters are mostly the unfinished things. They stay in the consciousness, and you carry it around with you. It may be un-forgiveness in your heart, some old memories, attachment to some old relationships or the gratitude in your heart that has not been expressed. It can be someone in your life who constantly brings you down with a negative attitude. It requires some courage and mindfulness to eliminate such mental clutters.

Like a clean, uncluttered home, a clutter free mind provides fresh energy into the life. If we are unaware, we cannot observe the clutters. However, if we are mindful we can always notice those clutters, and take action to eliminate them.

Benefits of de-cluttering:

Clutter creates obstructions in the flow of life energy. The stagnant energy that accumulates around these items over time creates corresponding stagnation in life. De-cluttering helps the life-energy move freely and in abundance in space and time. It promotes heath, happiness and prosperity. Clearing physical space also clears space in your mind, creating space for new ideas and opportunities. Clearing clutter is very satisfying. You will feel more relaxed, energized and more creative. It provides serenity, a balanced life, and harmonious relationships.

How to de-clutter?

Well, at first it may seem like a daunting task, when you take the first step, if you are not used to regular de-cluttering. Start small, but start in an area that will give you maximum impact for a limited time spent first. Maybe this is your kitchen. Start removing all those extra jars and bottles that occupy space for nothing. There may be some extra utensils that do not come to frequent use. Pack them up. Keep the counter spacious. Mindfully scan the place for every item that is not required. Do the same for the bathroom. Start by removing all items from the counter and around the tub. Replace just a couple of items that are most needed for everyday use. Pack up the rest of the things. If you are unable to throw them away, at least pack the items up and keep them in the cabinet for future use. But then, you need to de-clutter your cabinets once in a while.

Mindfully observe every room of your house. While looking at individual item notice your feelings. Is it pleasant, unpleasant or neutral? Identify the rooms that have maximum clutters. Make a room-by-room plan for de-cluttering. Drawing room and the bed room are very important; first remove the clutters from them. Take a basket and remove the excessive clutters.

After de-cluttering, leave the room and come back a little while later and take note of how you feel. You will see that it feels really good! Bit by bit, work your way around the house. It is a great idea to start a donation bag and a garbage bag.

After you are used to de-clutter for a while, you'll realize that you don't need half the stuff around you! Do not buy excess materials. Become aware about the impulse buying, when you visit the shopping malls. Buy only what you need. Before making a purchase, begin asking yourself these questions: Can you live without it? How will it benefit you? Do you have a place to store it?

Once you make de-cluttering a habit, it will be fun and relaxing. De-cluttering is a continuous process — not necessarily every day or week, but something that you can do regularly. A clean area motivates you to keep it that way, whereas a cluttered area invites more clutter. Hence, at the very first place try to keep your home clean and clutter-free. Develop a system that would keep your home clutter-free. Make it a habit to remove the excess materials. Once you have cleared the excess, you will be able to better discover which habits keep your living space free of clutter. And once you experience the freedom and stress-free life of living clutter-free, you will find these habits easier to maintain.

Similarly, to remove the digital cutters in your computers, laptops or smartphones, mindfully observe the applications that are no longer required, and remove them. You may have downloaded some apps a year ago and never used. Delete them. Remove all unnecessary digital files and documents that are no longer in use. Keep your email inbox at zero. After reading transfer the emails to appropriate folder and remove / archive the emails that are not required.

Mindfulness also helps you obtain a clutter-free mind. Clutter free mind is vital for happy living. Mindfully, notice your mind - your feelings. Are you carrying any stressful memory? If yes, allow it to let go. Release the clutters in your brain.

Clutter is the unaware luggage, the moment you drop it, you will jump into the higher energy orbit. You will feel free, lighter and happier. Mindfully notice these feelings. This will motivate you to remain clutter-free.

8. Mindful Posture Awareness

Mindfulness of posture is development of non-judgmental awareness of the body-postures during sitting, standing, walking, and lying down. It is noticing the positions of the arms, legs, ears, head, shoulders, elbows, hips, knuckles, back, spine and feet. It is observing the changing nature of the body postures. It is noticing the rising and falling nature of the body postures. Examine how all the body parts are changing their positions every time. Developing awareness about the body posture throughout the day trains the mind to know the unconscious habit patterns of the body.

Normally, we do not notice the movement of our body and the postures. Improper postural habits create stress and wear and tear in our bodies. Our body postures and our mental states are directly related. We are influenced by whatever mood or attitude our posture expresses. Because posture often expresses attitudes and emotions we are experiencing, attention to it can bring out a greater awareness of our underlying attitudes, moods, and feelings. For example, negative mental states such as fear, anger, and resistance are expressed in our posture quite differently than positive states like happiness, confidence, and determination. With some attitudes the body pulls in, rounds up, or tightens up, while with others, the body opens up, expands, and relaxes.

For example, if we slump when sad, the slumping can reinforce the sadness. If instead we assume an upright, strong and stable posture, not only are we less prone to sadness, we may be able to inspect sadness with a strong, stable awareness. If anxiety manifests in a tight chest, by sitting up straight with the chest wide open and shoulders rolled back, we are less likely to be under the influence of the anxiety. On the contrary, we'll feel confident and courageous to face the issue directly. We feel that we can take care of ourselves. Bringing awareness to the way we stand is also a powerful exercise we can build into our lives.

Before starting posture awareness you must be aware about the details of good posture and bad posture. Once you know that, you need to practice posture awareness time-to-time throughout the day, while sitting, standing, walking and lying down. At regular intervals during the day, take a moment to make a mental note of your posture. That awareness will transform bad posture into a good posture. This observation will reprogram your nervous system.

Whether you may be sitting at your desk, writing or typing at the keyboard, or standing in a queue, once you become aware of your posture, the body will automatically try to adjust its position and it will move form a bad posture to a good one. On the other hand, if you do not notice your posture, you create poor habits on a daily basis that most of the people don't even realize, which gradually contribute to pain in the future. Repetitive poor posture day after day, year after year will give one trouble sooner or later.

Good Posture:

Flexibility and relaxation is the key to good posture. Good posture involves proper alignment of the body parts while you are walking, standing, sitting or lying down. In good posture, least damage occurs on supporting muscles and ligaments during movement or weight-bearing activities. Gravity is continuously pulling our head and the body parts down. Good posture is maintaining the natural curvature of the spine with the head held high. And, as always, a good posture should not tense our body; it should be relaxed. When you are sitting on your office desk, typing, or reading something on your computer, make it a habit to notice often if your shoulders are tensed or relaxed. Mindfully relax your shoulders, upper back, lower back, the hip joint, and legs. Also take a mental note of your posture, while you are standing. If you can draw a line from your earlobe through your shoulder, hip, knee, to the middle of your ankle, it should align in one straight line. Relaxed and well balanced posture doesn't create damage to the body and creates least strain on supporting muscles and ligaments. Good posture is maintaining the natural curvature of the spine, keeping your back straight, shoulders back and tummy slightly in.

Poor Posture:

Poor posture is certain form of rigidity in the body parts, and muscles feel tightened. Poor posture affects the spine and the internal organs. If the spine and the internal organs are constantly misaligned, collapsed or compressed, they cannot function as they are intended for. Our spine and the main weight-bearing joints work best when aligned one on top of the other. Poor posture brings the shoulders in and pulls the head down, because as our shoulders roll forward, they drag everything forward, putting more weight on our neck and spine, joints and on our feet, and that makes the body out of balance.

Poor posture not only affects our musculoskeletal health but also dramatically decreases our overall performance. Mental states of low confidence, fear, anger, depression and resistance are often results of poor postures. Back pain, neck pain, digestive problems, respiratory problems, and chest tightness are often associated with poor postural habit. Poor posture closes the lungs, making it harder to breathe deep and stay relaxed.

Head forward, shoulders forward, rounded upper back, curved forward neck, depressed chest, rounded lower back, overstretched abdominals, pot bellies, abnormal rib-cage alignment, and altered spine curvature are examples of poor posture. Shoulder slumping is typically seen in a sitting position, whether at your office desk or at home. Long hours spent reading, watching television or staring at your computer can contribute to this habit. Pot bellies result when the lower back experiences an exaggerated curve, thus pushing the internal organs, in the abdominal region of the body, toward the front side of the body.

The average human head weighs about 4.5 kg, while it is straight on top of your spine. However, if you keep your head forward or backward, the pressure on your spine and shoulder muscles will increase due to the lever effect. This can force the muscles in your upper back and neck to work much harder to keep the head from dropping forwards onto your chest. This extra pressure adversely affects the nerves at the base of the skull. Moreover, forward head posture could result in as much as thirty percent loss of lung capacity. Poor posture is also a contributing factor to several digestive problems ranging from acid reflux to constipation and even liver disease and hernias. Your posture can be indicative of how you feel throughout the day. With a little mindfulness, you can be able to maintain a good posture, which is empowering. It can be a powerful tool for a happy and healthy life.

Posture Awareness

Take a moment from time to time to monitor your postures. Become aware of your body posture. Notice whether you are in standing, sitting, walking or lying down positions. How are you sitting or standing in this moment? How are the alignments of the rib cage? Is it bending backwards or flat? Pay attention to the positions of your body parts. Gradually observe the right hand position. Pay attention to the left hand position. Pay attention to your leg positions.

Examine the weight on your feet. How the weight is distributed on the feet? A good posture, maintains most of the weight on the balls of the feet and not on the heels. Is there tension in your shoulders, face, hands, or back?

Posture Awareness while Sitting

Our body is not designed to sit for long time. Avoid sitting in the same position for more than 30 minutes. While you sit on a chair, your lower back of your spinal cord should get optimum support.

- Sit up with your back straight and your shoulders back.
- Distribute your body weight evenly on both hips.
- Bend your knees at a right angle.
- Keep your feet flat on the floor.
- Adjust your chair height so that you can sit close to your work.

When you are ready to stand, move to the front of the seat, then stand up by straightening your legs.

Awareness of the correct neck and shoulder posture is the first step toward cultivating correct posture. Frequently take a mental note of the position of your neck and head. Where is your head? Does it come forward away from your shoulders? Or does it sit directly on top of your spine? Are your shoulders curved or rounded? Whatever it is just notice with an attitude of loving care, without judgment or disappointment. Notice if you are feeling comfortable or strained.

Posture Awareness While Standing

By keeping your body relaxed, and straight you can decrease several inches from the belly area. It increases the distance between your lower ribs and the hip bones, allowing greater volume for the internal organs to extend. This can instantaneously reduce an unattractive "pot belly" or a "Donald duck lower back."

Mindfully notice the positions of your head and the neck. Are they in the ideal positions? Are they well balanced and supported? Examine the position of the upper back and the spine. Make a mental note of the curvature of the upper back and the spine. Are your shoulders inclining forward? Notice the position of your chest. Inspect the lower back. Observe the gap between the feet. Notice the position of your feet. Is your body well supported?

Great posture will give you greater confidence in all that you do, and, it's queer but true, the taller you stand, the more respect you earn from the people around you. The taller you stand, the more focused you will be on your posture. The taller you stand the more balanced, secure and confident will you feel. And when you stand tall and upright you will naturally feel more reassured, serene and powerful, in all that you do. Bring every motion you do throughout the day under the lens of mindfulness. Keep your shoulders back, your chest and chin open and proud.

Happiness, confidence, determination and good health is the result of good posture. Good posture aligns your internal organs and spine in right position. Body language and posture go hand in hand. Good posture gives you confidence, self esteem and a sense of well-being.

Spinal Awareness:

While walking, standing, sitting or lying down, you can steadily maintain spinal awareness. Our spinal column is a complex, intricate construct that includes a variety of nerves, bones, joints, tendons, ligaments, and muscles woven together. Broadly, spine has three parts; the cervical spine (neck), the thoracic spine (upper-back and middle-back) and the lumbar spine (lower back). The spine is designed to be remarkably strong, with a great deal of flexibility in the lower back and neck area.

Mindfulness of the spine can be a great tool for improving your health and mental state. Feel often the sensations in your spine. Is it neutral, stressed, rigid or blissful? Is it curved, flat or normal? Your aim is not to control the spinal movements but just to observe it. Inspect the movements and bends of your spine while you may be doing your normal activities. Notice the movement of your lower back, middle back, upper back and the neck. Notice the curvatures of the spine at various areas. Are they normal? Don't try to do anything with your spine – simply notice it, pay attention to it and be aware of it. Allow your body to adjust what it will do naturally. The moment you start observing the position of the spine, you consciousness will change. Gradually your mind will be calm and quiet.

9. Mindful Walking

Walking is a great exercise to burn calories, lose weight, decrease stress, decrease blood pressure, improve bone health, and improve feelings of well being. Walking with correct form can strengthen weak muscles, stretch and relax the tight muscles, and improve breathing capacity and posture.

Through mindful walking, you bring your mind to the present moment and you thoroughly enjoy the moment, rather than wandering in thoughts. The first step of mindful walking is to bring your attention to your environment. See the beauty of the nature. See the trees, mountains, and the open sky. If you are walking on a city pathway, notice the road ahead, notice the buildings nearby and the sky above your head. Notice the colors, textures. If you are walking in a mall, notice the people, shops, colors and the sounds.

Be mindful to keep your head and neck relaxed and straight. Imagine someone is pulling you upward with a string attached to your head. Keep your chest forward. Imagine someone is pulling you forward with a string attached to your chest. Pretend you are two inches taller. Increase the distance between your hip bones and your rib cage. Swing arms deliberately in opposition to your legs. Slightly tighten and strengthen the abdominal muscles by pulling your belly button towards your spine.

Researchers observed that a walk in green and natural environments during the lunch time leads to better sleep and reduced blood pressure and stress. A brisk walk can reduce the risk of heart disease. Brisk walking boosts endorphins, which can reduce stress hormones.

Taking regular 20 to 30 minutes of mindful walking is great for health. Choose to walk in a peaceful area, around a lake, or along a trail in a park, instead of along a busy road, for instance.

While walk, avoid the drooping. Mindfully try to hold your head high, and stand tall and upright. Mindfully look forward, and not at the ground where you step on. Look about 20 feet ahead. This reduces strain on the neck and the back. Be mindful to maintain most of your weight on the balls of your feet and not on your heels. When you stand, the highest point of your body should be the top back region of your head. When you put your weight on your heels, you create misalignment in your body.

Mindfully scan your whole body while walking. Notice the tensions, feel the sensations in the body parts. You can start it with your head and continue with your shoulders, arms, chest, belly, hips, upper legs, lower legs, and feet. Observe the sensations from head to toe and toe to head. Slow down a little from time to time, and pay attention to how the muscles feel with the movements. For most people, the optimum walking speed is about 3 miles per hour. Notice your walking speed. Are you walking at slow, high or normal speed?

Pay attention to your footsteps, without looking at them. You may choose to count your footsteps as "one, two, three, four and so on." If you find your thoughts drifting elsewhere, simply bring it back to counting the footsteps. Paying attention to your footstep will keep you at the present moment.

You may also choose to focus your awareness on your breathing, as you walk. If persistent thoughts distract you from mindful walking, simply notice them, and then return to your breathing. Allow yourself to notice any sights, sounds, or physical sensations that may come up as you walk. Rest your awareness for a while on that sight, sound, or sensation, and then return your awareness to your breathing.

10. Mindful Eating

Mindful eating is paying attention to the present moment while eating. Open your awareness to whatever is arising at the moment. Being more mindful of eating enhances your health physically, emotionally and spiritually. Allow time to enjoy your food - the main sustainer of your life.

Pay attention to the surroundings and the environment. Notice the chairs, tables, dishes and the food arrangements. Look at your food with love and compassion. Observe all the items and the menus. You may notice your saliva secreting and impulses arise to urge you to eat the food. Notice the status of your stomach. Is it full or empty? Examine the colors, textures and forms of the foods. Notice the nature of the foods; whether it is soft, hard, coarse, or smooth.

You may take more time eating each part of your meal. Try not to read or talk at the same time. Take a bite, and mindfully notice the tastes and smells of the food you are eating. Is it sweet, bitter, sour, salty or pungent? Examine how your body responds to such tastes. Notice the aroma. Examine the smell of the food. What type of smell is that? Is it pleasant, unpleasant or neutral?

Pay attention to the touches of the food in your fingers and mouth. Notice the pressure, temperature, and the movement of the food in your mouth. Is the feeling pleasant, unpleasant or neutral? Examine how your mind responds to such taste. Are you relaxed or tensed?

Notice when your mind wanders away from the activity of eating, and mindfully bring it back to eating your meal. Take the taste of every bite. Become fully present.

Time to time examine your thoughts. What thoughts does this food bring to mind? Is it memories or beliefs, pleasures or fears? If you find yourself zoned out when you eat, stop eating for a moment. Notice where your mind wanders; gently bring it back to eating. Experience the touch of food on your fingers. Explore the sensations of it in your mouth. Examine the sensations of the food moving down to your throat and on its way to your stomach. Is it hot, warm, or cold, hard or soft?

Notice and listen to your body's needs. If you feel full, then stop eating. After you've finished eating, take a few moments to enjoy the food before washing up or doing another activity. Take some deep breaths to savor the activity you have just finished.

11. Mindful Sleeping

Sleep is Natures wonderful gift to rejuvenate ourselves. It is a welcome respite from a hectic day, and most of us head to our bed without any mindfulness. We often unknowingly carry to our bed our worry about the next day's work, some incomplete office job, an argument with a colleague or a family member, or frustration about a day that didn't quite go our way.

It is good to prepare before sleep. Try to get rid of all vain thoughts or unnecessary thoughts of the day at job or workplace, and mindfully prepare for the most important time of your day, because sleep is preparation for the next day. A good night's sleep re-energizes, revitalizes and nourishes your body and mind. It removes the toxins from the body and brain cells. Have something warm to drink, like milk or herbal drink, which might relax you before bed. Make a point to switch off all strong lights and switch on only soft gentle lights at least one hour before going to bed. This preparation ensures sufficient secretion of the sleep hormone melatonin, which in turn relaxes your biological system. Put out the lamps when you go to bed. Dark environment is good for sleep. It does not disrupt the circadian rhythm.

Before going to sleep it is good to wash the hands, feet and face. It is excellent to massage the feet with a little oil. Sleeping on the right side is relaxing, and it activates the left nostril, which cools and relaxes the body. Sleeping on the left side helps digestion. It promotes the functioning of the right nostril and is good for health.

For optimum blood circulation, we should sleep on the left or right side of our body for 50% of our sleeping time and rest of the time we should change our position. Sleeping in the same position night after night can develop pain in neck and shoulder. You need to change your sleeping positions two to three times in the night, so that your blood flow or breathing is not restricted.

Don't cover the face while sleeping so that you can breathe properly. Otherwise a person breathes their own deoxidized air. The level of the head should be above that of the feet.

12. Mindful Attitudes

Our attitudes are important. Attitude to your life, your work, your colleagues, friends or family determines your relationship to them, and that in turn determines your life experience. Life brings up multiple occasions where jerk reactions, impatience or anger may seem like automatic or obvious course of action, though you might regret it later. We need to be mindful to cultivate an attitude of patience, compassion and equanimity. Together they comprise a state of warmhearted and connected presence during difficult moments in our lives.

Patience makes you strong and overcome many hindrances. Greater patience is a product of perfect mindfulness, which opens us to the present moment, so we can accept our experience with greater ease. Compassion provides emotional strength and resilience.

Equanimity allows you to absorb any shock whatsoever and fight back.

Mindfulness of our attitude allows us to select our course of action wisely, to our advantage. Becoming mindful helps us to acknowledge our shortcomings, forgive ourselves, motivate ourselves with kindness to care for ourselves and others, and be fully human. Recently growing number of research clearly demonstrates that compassion is related to emotional wellbeing, lower anxiety and depression, maintenance of healthy habits such as diet and exercise, and more satisfying personal relationships. Kindness opens our hearts to suffering of our fellow beings. When we open us to others, we know that we aren't alone. This creates a meaningful life experience.

13. Mindful Goal Setting and Planning

We should have goal in life, because without goal we cannot succeed in life. It is said; "A man without a goal is like a ship without a rudder."- Thomas Carlyle. When we have a goal, we feel more in control in life. By setting our goals we can focus our energy and it is easy for us to move forward. Mindful goal setting helps us to focus one task at a time.

There are two types of goals: routine goals and the creative goals. The routine goals are like sleeping, eating, showering, ironing, house cleaning, driving, going office at time, writing emails and other unchallenging normal activities of life. Mindfulness helps us to perform these routine activities with awareness and calmness. When we do these routine goals mindfully and peacefully we get more energy and more time for fulfilling the more challenging goals. The creative goals are the life-enriching goals. These give us the chances to realize our dreams. These may be goals around health, wellness, career, finance, love, family, building new house, project work, art work, new ventures, adventures, social service etc. In goal setting we are often too much driven by the experiences and fears of the past failures. Similarly, sometimes we are overconfidence about the future. Mindfulness gives us the deep insights about the realities.

Mindfulness helps us to set our goals realistic, inspiring, valuable and enjoyable. Even with specific goals and deadlines it's easy to get lost in the busy-ness of the routine works. Mindfulness keeps us focused and gently brings us back to the track. Instead of setting strict goals mindfulness helps us to create conditions that will likely to achieve the goals. Focusing on the goals every day is important, but outcomes can often be threatening, ambitious, and at their worst, downright discouraging. Mindfulness helps us to keep focus on the things that actually have to do to achieve the goals rather than on the emotions and the worry.

Mindfulness helps us to focus on one goal at a time. We should be more relaxed, patience and compassionate towards the goal. Too much attachment to goals creates problem. Often, we have limited control over the circumstances which could result in the plan changing. Through mindfulness, we can be more open to the changes and therefore able to handle things in a more calm and clear state of mind. Mindfulness gives more flexibility and adaptability.

Goal of enlightenment is the highest goal. In reality, you are always in the present moment. You are making your goals in the present moment. Present moment means we should be aware what we are doing in the moment. If we are feeling worry, anger or something like that we should be aware about that. We should be free from grasping or aversion about the goals.

Mindfulness takes away our energy from fear, unnecessary speculation or worry, and makes it available for flowering our dreams. Mindfully define your goal and know the path to that goal. Know what it is you wish to accomplish, and mindfully move towards that goal. Don't chase the goal but beautify your actions. The spirit is important.

Part –III

Micro-Mindfulness Meditation

We live in a busy world, and many of us don't have time to formally practice mindfulness skills. However, we can practice Micro-mindfulness throughout the day. Mindfulness is not ignoring our daily problems. It is solving the problems with equanimity, focus and clarity of mind. Micro-mindfulness meditations require small periods of mindfulness that we can incorporate into our daily lives. They can be done anywhere. They can be as brief as a few seconds. Through micro mindfulness, you will be utilizing your energies more efficiently. When you pay attention to the job at hand, instead of being lost in the past and future thoughts, you will be solving your problems with much peace, happiness and accuracy. Micro-mindfulness will help you to recognize the elements of happiness already present in your life.

The micro-mindfulness practice involves reminding ourselves throughout the day to pay attention to what is happening in the moment, without drastically altering our normal routines. It may be just observing the position of your hands, legs, neck or head. It may be noticing the sensations in the body or noticing the feelings of relaxation while just consciously stretching the body a little bit. It may be noticing the exhalation of your breath for a few seconds. It may be just relaxing the shoulder muscles, consciously, and observing the feeling of relaxation. It may be consciously observing a tree, a bird, the open sky or the surroundings, sensing their presence. It may be consciously feeling the sensations in the tongue while eating. You may perform your favorite yoga mudras (postures of your eyes, tongue and fingers) for a few seconds, and observe the position of your fingers. While working on the computer, you may just mindfully change the hand you are using to control the mouse. Use the hand that you normally do not use. You may use your normally unused hand to brush your teeth for a few moments. You may try to read something from right to left rather than from the left to right, for a few seconds. While walking, consciously you may take a few steps larger or smaller than your normal steps, while observing the process mindfully. These are just a few examples. You can improvise it in thousands of ways. There is no end to the opportunities where you can practice mini-mindfulness. You can make use of every small opportunity to break the typical habitual patterns of the mind. These small meditations can stop the mental and emotional inertia, in an almost effortless manner.

Just one thing is necessary for the practice. These micro-mindfulness meditations should be performed with very little activity and these practices should not be associated with any goal, concept or belief. After performing the Micro mindfulness meditation, release the energy of your mind and body for your normal activity. Such Micro meditation consists of focusing your awareness to perform a single task consciously for a small fraction of time, while mindfully observing the process. This may sound too simplistic, but it has profound effects on the body and mind because it frequently clears the fog of the mind and keeps you clear headed, sharp and focused. It actually cuts through the unconscious habitual patterns and the silly and obsessive thoughts of the mind.

Think back of the last long meditation you did where a lot of efforts were made for stilling the body and the mind. Micro mindfulness will quickly train your mind to remain focused.

When you encounter a problem in life, do you generally turn to look at your bodily sensations or feelings first, or do you jump in to the problem? Normally, if you do not already have more than 200 hours of mindfulness meditation practice, you will look at the problem first. However, these micro meditation practices will develop your awareness of your feelings in every situation of life, especially in the midst of emotional turmoil. These techniques will keep your mind sharp, clear and balanced. These techniques will help you to develop stability. They will develop in you a tendency to act from fresh and aware mind instead of reacting from stale beliefs, memory and fear. These can be practiced while you are doing other things, at the time of breaks or intervals during your office works, household duties or other commitments.

Micro-Mindfulness practices

A few examples of Micro-mindfulness practice are given below:

1. Micro-Mindfulness: Five Deep Breathings

Drop for a while whatever you are doing or thinking, to practice this. This micro mindfulness practice will help you to quickly centre yourself and connect with your environment.

1. Take five slow, deep breaths, keeping your mouth shut. Focus on breathing out as slowly as possible until the lungs are completely empty, and then allow them to refill by themselves.

2. Notice the sensations of your lungs emptying. Notice the feeling of relaxation as the breath goes out. Notice how your shoulders and rib cage are falling as you exhale out.

3. If any thoughts come, let them pass by, just as the traffic on the road pass by your car, when you drive, and bring your awareness back to your breathing.

4. After you finish five breaths, look around the room and notice what you can see, hear, smell, touch, and feel.

5. Resume your normal activities.

You can practice it anytime throughout the day, especially when you find yourself off-center and caught up in repetitive thoughts and feelings.

2. Micro-Mindfulness: Awareness of the Things around You

When you find your mind too busy with some unnecessary internal chatter, worry or anxiety, you can come out of it with this simple practice of micro mindfulness.

1. Take a deep breath, exhale slowly, and smile. Do it three times. Drop whatever you are doing to pause for a moment.

2. Look around and notice. Take note of whatever catches your attention first. Look at it as if you are seeing it for the first time. It may be your phone, it may be your laptop, it may be a bottle of water, or the fan moving over your head. It may be a tree outside the window, a bird, or a fly! Whatever it is, don't try to analyze. Just look at it as if you are looking at it for the first time. Notice the color, texture and the form in minute details.

3. Listen carefully, and notice any sound you can hear. It may be a song, the buzzing sound of a motor, a conversation going on nearby, or anything else. Don't analyze. Just listen to the sound. If there are several sounds in your environment, become aware of as many of them as you can, and listen very attentively for a minute or two.

4. Observe the feeling of touch in your body. Place your feet on the floor. Feel the floor in contact with your feet. Feel the contact of your shirt with your skin, feel your trousers against your legs. Feel the air on your face. Feel the

contact of your tongue against the upper palate.

5. Finally, become aware of your whole environment. Try to feel the throb of life in every activity going on around you. Take a deep breath, smile and return to your job.

3. Micro-Mindfulness with Earth Touching

Touching the Earth is a great way to remove anxiety and come back to yourself. It immediately has a grounding effect on you. It anchors you in the moment. This exercise is best practiced in a natural setting on green grass filled lawn, meadow, garden or park.

1. Remove your shoes and stand on the earth barefoot. Place your feet squarely on the ground.

2. Close your eyes for a second and feel the ground below you.

3. Open your eyes and take a slow long breath. Exhale slowly, and feel the earth.

4. Inhale and fill your body with Prana, the vital energy that resides in breath. Exhale, and release all the vain thoughts, worries and anxieties. You can say it in your mind, if you like, with every inhalation and exhalation. Inhaling, I fill my body with life energy; exhaling, I relax and let go of tensions in my body and mind. Do it for five breaths.

5. Walk a few steps on the ground, if you like. Feel the nourishing presence of mother earth holding you and nourishing your body and mind.

Part IV

Formal Mindfulness Meditations

1. Breath Meditation

The easiest way to start a mindfulness meditation is to focus on your breath. Breath is the indicator of our emotional state. By focusing on the breath we get in sync with our breath. It slows down the chattering of mind that always goes on the background of everything you are doing. Meditation on breath strengthens the mental muscles. As we focus on breath, we develop a relaxed rhythm of breathing.

This exercise takes about 20 minutes. Set your alarm clock accordingly. The sound of alarm should be very soft, so it doesn't startle you when the session is over. Arrange your environment. Keep it private, quite and comfortable. Sit down in a comfortable position with your back straight and gently supported but let the spine maintain its natural curve. Keep the body comfortable and relaxed. If you are sitting on a chair, put your feet flat on the floor with your legs uncrossed. Keep your head and neck balanced. Keep your hands on your knees. Relax your hands. Make sure that your hands are supported so that there is no strain in your shoulders. Relax your jaw, eyes, and the forehead. Soften your gaze, and then gently close your eyes.

Now bring your attention to your breathing. Observe the quality of the incoming and outgoing breath in details. Feel the sensation of air flowing in and out of your nostrils. Feel the expansion of your lungs, rib cages, chest and belly as you breathe in. Focus your awareness on where the sensations are the strongest.

Pay attention to where you notice your breathing most easily. Some people feel it mostly at the nostrils. Other people can feel the chest rising and falling. Still others feel the breath most clearly in the abdomen area, as the belly expands with inhalation and contracts with exhalation. Gently explore your body and discover where your breathing sensation is easiest to notice.

Notice the cool sensations of the in breath and the warm sensations of the out breath. Don't control the breath in any way. Let it flow naturally. Be kind, compassionate and loving towards the breath. It is life force coming within you and detoxifying the body when it is going out.

Enjoy your breathing. It is not a method of concentration; just keep a relaxed awareness of the breath. You are not your breath. You are the watcher of your breath. Make no effort to change the rhythm of your breathing. In the beginning, it is often difficult to maintain the awareness of breathing. Mental volitions and other thoughts may interfere with your breathing awareness. No matter whatever thought arises gently bring the awareness back to breathing. Stay focused on nothing except the sensation of the air flowing in and out of your nostrils or any place where the breathing sensations are felt. As soon as a thought comes into your mind, just notice it, and let it go, without following it. Come back and pay attention to the sensations of the flow of air.

Allow yourself sufficient time for doing this breathing awareness meditation. You can do it for ten minutes or you can do it for an hour, depending on your availability of time. Gradually your breathing will become very slow and subtle, and your mind, quiet. Gently open the eyes, when the session is over.

2. Breath Meditation Type II

Like we have discussed in the previous section, after you have set your timer and adjusted your sitting position, bring your attention to your breathing. Observe the quality of the incoming and outgoing breath in details. Feel the sensation of air flowing in and out of your nostrils. Focus your awareness on where the breathing sensations are the strongest.

Pay attention to where you notice your breathing most easily. After you have identified the area where it is easiest for you to notice the breathing sensation, try to find out which is easier for you to notice, the in-breath or the out-breath. Most people find it easier to focus either on the in-breath or on the out-breath, rather than focusing on both simultaneously. Choose one, either in-breath or the out-breath as your object of focus. Let us assume that you chose exhalation and that the area of focus you selected was the nostrils.

Focus your attention on the feeling of exhalation. Feel the air coming out of your nostrils each time you exhale. Is it warm, or hot? Is it short or long? Do not pay attention to inhalation that takes place immediately after exhalation; let it take place automatically. Be spacious, open and silent to accommodate the overall experience of your being and then feel your breath again as your body exhales. Let the process be effortless, as if your body is breathing you. You are just an impartial observer. Simply pay attention to the sensation of the air in your nose each time you exhale, one breath after another.

Be aware how your breath nourishes and purifies you whether you are paying attention to it or not. Like a loving mother it feeds your body and cleans it. Your mind will wander away from the sensation of the breath many times every minute. Don't worry about how often your mind wanders. Gently return to the feeling of your breathing when you notice that your mind has wandered. After 15 or 20 minutes, gently open your eyes and savor the stillness of the moment before moving on.

3. Mindfulness of Body Sensations

Mindfulness of body sensations is one of the most effective meditation techniques. It can easily ground your mind in the present moment.

This exercise takes about thirty minutes. Please find a quiet, comfortable place to sit. Set your alarm clock. For these thirty minutes, do not allow the body to move. Keep it as still as possible. But keep it relaxed and flexible. Get connected with the present.

Take three, slow easy deep breaths to relax and let go of whatever burdens you're carrying around. Then let your eyelids gently close, or partially close, which ever makes you more comfortable. Form an image of yourself sitting down. Note your posture on the chair as if you were seeing yourself from the outside.

Now bring your attention inside your body and feel the pulsation and vibration of your body. Just feel the sensations for a minute. Let them be just as they are, pleasant, unpleasant, or neutral.

Use the body-parts as the objects of awareness and return your attention back to the body sensations each time the mind wonders. Observe the sensations like warmth, coldness, touch of the cloth, touch of air, heaviness, lightness, numbness, pain, pleasure, throbbing, tingling and so on. Observe the body sensations with utmost equanimity, without attachment or aversion.

List of the body parts are given below. While meditating, you can mentally utter the name of the body parts. Spend a few moments with the feelings of that body part. Move your awareness to the next body part and observe the feelings of that part. Rotate your awareness throughout the body slowly, from the toe to the head and from the head to the toe, according to the list (from 1 to 17 and then from 17 to 1). Hold your attention on each part for sufficient time to feel the sensations. Do not sleep. Know each of your body cells. Understand their feeling. Identify the cells that are happy. Identify the cells that are not so happy at the moment. Observe how sensations are changing. Give hundred percent attentions to the feelings of the cells. Each of your cells is waiting for your attention. Give attention to each of your cell. Do not neglect any one. All are equally important. All the cells are living beings, having their own personality. By your attention, you are loving and nurturing them.

Following are the names of the body parts, which you may mentally utter, while moving your attention from one part to another.

1. Right foot
2. Left foot
3. Right calf
4. Left calf
5. Right thigh
6. Left thigh
7. Hips
8. Stomach
9. Chest
10. Back
11. Spine
12. Right arm and hand
13. Left arm and hand
14. Neck and shoulders
15. Face
16. Brain
17. Skull

Put your loving attention on the physical sensations such as itching, tingling, aching, tightness, warmth, coldness, heaviness, lightness, and also note any emotional experiences that manifest in the mind.

Regardless of your experience, hold your awareness on the present moment, with an attitude of acceptance. Try to notice these physical sensations without judging them, holding on to them or trying to push them away. Do not be carried away by the thoughts or emotions. Do not bring in to practice any other meditation techniques like chanting or visualization of a chosen object. Don't label any experience and don't interpret. Just feel the raw sensations as they are. Observe the stillness of the body. Observe the stillness of the mind. You should rotate your awareness throughout the body without getting stuck at any part.

Stay with the experience of relaxation and calmness of the mind, as long as you can. Do this as long as you are comfortable. If want to make movements in your body parts. Make the movement and make a note of it.

4. Feeling Awareness Meditation

Sit quietly for a few minutes with your back straight, maintaining the natural curve of the spine. Let your body relax. Open your awareness to whatever is arising at the present moment.

Focus your awareness on your breathing. Breathe normally and gently through your nose. Allow your breathing to follow its natural course. Do not try to force or change the natural pattern of your breathing. As you feel each breath, carefully recognize it with the words “in-breath”, or “out-breath,” saying the words silently and softly at the back of your mind. You may find yourself spontaneously taking longer or shorter breaths at different times. Allow this to happen and be aware of these changes as they occur. Continue paying attention on your breathing until any strong experience arises to interrupt your attention. If you have strong feelings, notice your feelings — pleasant, unpleasant or neutral. Focus your total attention on it.

There are two types of feelings — positive feelings and negative feelings. Depression, frustration, fear, sadness, anxiety, anger, jealousy, hatred and hurt are negative feelings. Happiness, confidence, peace, joy etc. are positive feelings. Examine the type of feelings you have. Positive feelings generate a sense of ease and pleasure; it is easier to deal with them. If you have very peaceful, joyful and happy feelings, pay attention to the feelings as it is. Give your total attention to it. Notice the rising, continuation and the passing away of the feelings. Do not react to the positive feelings with attachments. Don't try to make it everlasting. If the positive feelings vanishes, don't get upset; simply accept the fading away. Welcome the process as it is. Experience the feelings right now with a gentle, non-judgmental and non-reactive way.

Negative feelings are much difficult to manage. If a strong negative feeling arises during your meditation, don't try to reject it or push it away prematurely. Cultivate patience with unpleasant feelings. It takes time for any feeling to go away. Gradually ground yourself by paying attention to your body parts. Notice that during the negative feelings your body becomes tense. Your mind becomes agitated and heart contracts. Feel your body with full awareness and kindness.

Notice the places of tension or holding of emotions as tightness or strain. If any feelings of guilt arise, forgive yourself for your mistakes and shortcomings. Painful memories or hurtful thoughts are not always easy to go. If you cannot eliminate negative emotions immediately, you can change your relationship with them. Become loving to yourself, and your feelings. Like everything in this existence they too have a reason to exist. With your loving attention they will gradually melt away.

It is helpful to remember that feelings do not come from the object that you perceive but from your mental state or mental attitude. Remind yourself that you are not your feelings. You are the observer of your feelings. Remain focused on the feelings in the body not with the connected thoughts. Do not react to the negative feelings with aversion.

Observe the painful feelings with patience in order to pursue the long-term rewards of a peaceful and balanced mind. The more you remain patient and aware, the more you become aware of the unconscious cycle of reaction within you. The more you become aware of the unconscious cycle of reaction within you, the more is the possibility of your getting rid of them. The more you get rid of the unconscious cycle of reaction within you, the more peace and joy will flow within you, and ultimately you'll be able to reap the long-term reward of a balanced, stable and peaceful mind that nothing can disturb. Such a mind is the treasure of a Buddha.

Continue this practice for as long as you wish (about 10-15 minutes is a good period to start with). The skill of equanimity will gradually develop; it depends upon your ability to detach from the feelings. You can develop the skill by practicing mindfulness of feelings, whenever you have a few minutes at your disposal.

5. Posture Meditation

Mindfulness of posture is an important foundation for meditation. Mindfulness of posture may help us know how a particular posture can be improved in subtle ways. It is important to give careful attention to physical discomfort that arises in meditation.

During meditation, subtle shifts in posture can indicate a change of our psychological state. Tension arising in the mind during meditation can translate into tensed body or posture. Stability, confidence and resilience of mind can be more readily available when we assume postures that give these qualities a chance to appear. Mindful postures enhance awareness of our body by bringing a greater sense of embodiment or grounding. In addition, they help prevent unnecessary discomfort in meditation.

Body posture and mind are closely linked. If your body is simple, upright, strong, and open, your mind will tend to be like that. We need a good posture not only during the formal sitting meditations; we need it throughout the day. In fact posture awareness can itself become a highly effective practice of meditation. Again, you can practice posture awareness meditation before beginning any other type of meditation.

Posture awareness meditation can be practiced sitting cross legged, or on a chair with the feet placed flat on earth side by side, a little apart. This exercise may take about fifteen minutes. Please find a quiet, comfortable place to sit. Set your alarm clock. For these fifteen minutes, do not allow the body to move. Keep it as still as possible. But keep it relaxed and flexible.

Ground yourself to this moment by taking three, slow deep breaths. Relax and let go of whatever burdens you're carrying in your mind. Then let your eyelids gently close, or partially close, which ever makes you more comfortable. Form an image of yourself sitting down. Note your posture on the chair, or on the ground on your meditation cushion, as if you were seeing yourself from the outside. Mentally observe the body slowly from head to feet. Mentally observe the position of your hands. Observe the positions of your legs. Observe the curve of your spine. Finally, observe the full body. Mentally observe your sitting posture. Feel your body and its posture. Are you sitting with your back straight? Or, are you slumping? Are your shoulders drooping forward? Is your neck carrying your head straight on it, or does your head tilt forward? Your body will automatically go on correcting its position as you notice your posture.

First mentally observe yourself from the front, then from the back, from the left, from the right, from the bottom, and from the top. Observe your body as if you are observing someone else from outside. Observe every details, every bend. How does your body look like when you are meditating? Feel the body as a whole and note the physical discomfort that arises during meditation. You may want to make a slight change in your posture to make yourself more comfortable. Do so very slowly, noticing every tiny change in the position of your hands, legs, spine, neck and head.

Finally notice your breath again. See how a comfortable posture makes your breaths smoother and easy flowing. Continue this practice for as long as you wish.

Part V

Flowering of Mindfulness

Mindfulness helps us realize the impermanent nature of everything. Mindfulness gives us the opportunity to realize the non-self nature of our mental formations, thoughts and emotions. When we realize impermanence as the real destiny of things, and non-self nature of thoughts and things, this understanding makes us more compassionate and kind. Go to the center of your heart and spread love in every direction - without any specific target - without any boundary.

We can beautify every moment just by changing our attitude towards life. Compassion, love, equanimity, non-attachment, awareness and alertness are the fabrics of beauty. The journey of compassion starts with the self. Mindfulness helps us change our attitude towards the life and self.

We are not islands. We are deeply interconnected with people, society and the environment. Mindfulness helps us to develop a more aware and compassionate connection to ourselves, others and the world. Mindfulness gives us greater understanding, awareness, sensitivity, and respect towards people, environment and the society. Collaboration is the essence of life. In Nature, the wind, bees and flowers work together, to spread the pollens. The bees collect pollen and nectar from the flower. The capacity of the bee is limited in many ways but she travels from flower to flower without stress or hurry. She is in search of the sweetest, most attractive nectar. Once the stomach is full with nectar the bee returns to the hive. At the same time she also spread the pollens automatically. Mindfulness gives us the understanding of the cosmic collaboration. When we think us disconnected, we develop stress in our being. Mindfulness makes us understand the interconnectedness of all things and beings. It makes our life flowery. We need to focus on the flowering, and not on the bees. We need to focus on the beautification of our action, and not much on the results. When flowering is perfect bees will come.

Our adventures and our dreams are the glory of our soul. We are here to fulfill our unique dreams. We are here to fly on the open sky with our wings wide and open. Magic lies outside the nest – outside the comfort zone. Mindfulness gives us the courage, confidence and humility to walk on the edge - outside the comfort zone. Mindfulness helps us to walk on the edge, as well as relax at the middle. We are here to make this tiny life glorious. And to make this life glorious, we need to dive out of the comfort zone. In this dive mindfulness works like parachutes. It releases all the load of the past and the future. Mindfulness is the safety belt to swim in the ocean of uncertainties. Mindfulness keeps us safe.

Mindfulness helps us travel through the secret path of kindness and happiness – the path of paradise. Instead of thinking all the time - learn to listen the music of the moment. Mind is a flexible mirror; adjust it, to see a better world. Our adventures, creativity and independence are vital for our growth and evolution. Mindfulness makes us aware and conscious about them. It teaches us to nourish them in a positive way – in a conscious way. It helps us to take risk and shows us ways where there is no path. Mindfulness teaches us to embrace change and turn the challenges into opportunities. Successful leaders don't wait for change to appear - they invite the change with mindfulness. Mindfulness keeps them ahead of the change.

You don't need to change the world. The world is continuously changing. You just need to ride and enjoy the changes. You just need to take leverage of that change. Never walk behind the change. Walk around and in front of the change. Mindfulness is the art of riding the change. Mindfulness gives us alarm much before the storm - much before the change. It helps to stay much ahead of the changes. Changes are like wild horses. We just need to learn the art of riding them with patience and tranquility.

About the Author

Dr. Amit Ray is an author, philosopher and spiritual master. He teaches peace, love and compassion for the transformation of human consciousness. He is author of several books on meditation and yoga.

In his early years, he was a scientist. He did his PhD in artificial intelligence and computational neuroscience and worked as a scientist in India, UK and USA. With a spiritual bent of mind from his very childhood, he undertook intense practices in meditation from his early years. In his later years, many mystical experiences prompted him to dedicate his life for the search of truth.

He began sharing his experiences after a series of transformative spiritual awakening. In his Himalayan centre, he lives a life dedicated to meditation, yoga and transformation of human consciousness.

Also from Inner Light Publishers

Awakening Inner Guru:

Awakening Inner Guru is a clear and straightforward guide to awaken the light within. For those who are truly interested to attain spiritual freedom and fulfillment in every sphere of life, this book is a practical and personal manual. ISBN: 9788191026900

Om Chanting and Meditation

Om is our blissful Self. Om is the mysterious cosmic energy that is the substratum of all the things and all the beings. It is the eternal song of the Divine. This book makes the Om meditation easy to follow, simple to do, and very effective. ISBN: 9788191026931

Yoga and Vipassana: An Integrated Lifestyle

Vipassana Meditation and Yoga are integrated and combined together in this book in a coherent manner. This is intended for those people who want to explore and utilize the benefits of the two ancient techniques of yoga and vipassana in a seamless manner. It is planned for developing deep wisdom, great calmness and joy in life. ISBN: 9788191026924

Laughing Buddha: The Alchemy of Euphoric Living

The spirit of Laughing Buddha is the spirit of ultimate relaxation, happiness and contentment. This book gives a rare combination of ancient Buddhist wisdom and its practical use in our daily lives in the modern world for living in joy. ISBN: 9788191026948

Affirmations and Visualizations: The Ultimate Secret

This is a practical and comprehensive guidebook for affirmation and visualization that contains a wealth of practical information, tips, instructions and exercises for improving your life. You will know how and at which level of your mind affirmations and visualization work. You will know the scientific and esoteric secret of working of your mind and how to train your mind to unleash your hidden power. ISBN: 9789382123156

We at Inner Light Publishers are dedicated to publish books that help to improve the quality of human lives. You are welcome to visit us at www.inner-light-in.com